15 Ways to Increase Your Earnings

From the Qur'ān and Sunnah

Abu Ammaar Yasir Qadhi

ISBN 1 898649 56 1

British Library Cataloguing in Publication Data.

A catalogue record for this book is available from the British Library.

Published: Al-Hidaayah Publishing and Distribution

Distributed by: Al-Hidaayah Publishing and Distribution
P.O. Box 3332
Birmingham
United Kingdom
B10 0UH

Tel: 0121 753 1889
Fax: 0121 753 2422
Website: www.al-hidaayah.co.uk
Email: mail@al-hidaayah.co.uk

ٱلْمَالُ وَٱلْبَنُونَ زِينَةُ ٱلْحَيَوٰةِ ٱلدُّنْيَا ۖ وَٱلْبَٰقِيَٰتُ ٱلصَّٰلِحَٰتُ
خَيْرٌ عِندَ رَبِّكَ ثَوَابًا وَخَيْرٌ أَمَلًا ﴿٤٦﴾

Wealth and children are the adornments of the life of this world; but the permanent righteous deeds are better in your Lord's Sight (to attain) rewards, and better in respect of hope.

Sūrah *al-Kahf*, verse 46

How admirable is pure money for a pious man!

Prophetic ḥadīth

The money that a true believer needs to support himself with is comparable to the donkey that he rides, and the carpet that he sits on - nay, rather the toilet that he relieves himself in - for he has a need for these things, but they do not occupy a status (in his heart)...

Shaykh al-Islām Ibn Taymiyyah

15 Ways to Increase Your Earnings
From the Qur'ān and Sunnah

Contents

Transliteration Table

Consonants,

ء	'	د	d	ض	ḍ	ك	k
ب	b	ذ	dh	ط	ṭ	ل	l
ت	t	ر	r	ظ	ẓ	م	m
ث	th	ز	z	ع	ʿ	ن	n
ج	j	س	s	غ	gh	ه	h
ح	ḥ	ش	sh	ف	f	و	w
خ	kh	ص	ṣ	ق	q	ي	y

Vowels, diphthongs, etc.

Short:	ـَ	a	ـِ	i	ـُ	u
Long:	ـَا	ā	ـِي	ī	ـُو	ū
diphthongs:			ـَيْ	ay	ـَوْ	aw

Foreword

All praise is due to Allāh, who blessed mankind with comforts in this life, and made these comforts a reward exclusively for His servants in the hereafter, for He said,

قُلْ مَنْ حَرَّمَ زِينَةَ ٱللَّهِ
ٱلَّتِىٓ أَخْرَجَ لِعِبَادِهِۦ وَٱلطَّيِّبَٰتِ مِنَ ٱلرِّزْقِ ۚ قُلْ هِىَ لِلَّذِينَ ءَامَنُوا۟
فِى ٱلْحَيَوٰةِ ٱلدُّنْيَا خَالِصَةً يَوْمَ ٱلْقِيَٰمَةِ ۗ

> "Say: Who has forbidden the adoration with clothes given by Allāh, which He has produced for his slaves, and the good [and pure] food? Say: They are, in the life of this world, for those who believe, (and) exclusively for them on the Day of Resurrection." [Sūrah *al-Aʿrāf*, 32]

And peace and blessings be upon the final Prophet and Messenger, Muḥammad ibn ʿAbdillāh (ﷺ), who said,

> "How admirable is pure money for a righteous person!" [1]

---

[1] The *takhrīj* of this ḥadīth will be discussed later. Throughout this work, I have tried to do an exhaustive *takhrīj* of all the *aḥadīth* quoted, hoping that this might add benefit to the work. (The science of *takhrīj* involves mentioning the primary source book in which a ḥadīth has been narrated, along with a discussion of the authenticity of the ḥadīth. For the authenticity, I restricted myself to quoting the various scholars of the field who have established themselves as authorities on this subject. Where the ḥadīth was recorded by al-Bukhārī or Muslim, I did not, in general, quote other references, as the presence of a ḥadīth in one of these two books is sufficient proof for its authenticity.)

As to what follows, Allāh has created mankind and blessed him with supervision of many other elements of His creation. Furthermore, He has given mankind privileges that He has not granted any other creature, for He states,

وَلَقَدْ كَرَّمْنَا بَنِيٓ ءَادَمَ وَحَمَلْنَٰهُمْ
فِي ٱلْبَرِّ وَٱلْبَحْرِ وَرَزَقْنَٰهُم مِّنَ ٱلطَّيِّبَٰتِ وَفَضَّلْنَٰهُمْ عَلَىٰ
كَثِيرٍ مِّمَّنْ خَلَقْنَا تَفْضِيلًا ﴿٧٠﴾

> "And Indeed We have honoured the Children of Ādam, and We have carried them over land and sea, and We have provided them with lawful (and pure) things. And We have preferred them above many of those whom We have created with a marked preference!" [Sūrah *al-Isrā*, 70]

One of the blessings that Allāh has given His servants is that of a convenient means of financial exchange, i.e. money. Money has since grown to become one of the most prized possessions of mankind, and like so many elements of the *dunya*, serves to test the obedience of Allāh's servants by challenging their system of priorities. Some may use this blessing to the benefit of themselves and of others, spending in a prudent manner pleasing to the One Who placed the money in their hands to begin with. Others may misuse this most beautiful gift of Allāh, thus incurring Allāh's displeasure, or even wrath and condemnation.

Therefore, due to the fact that the Muslims of today are preoccupied with the seeking of money to an extent almost unparalleled in Islāmic history, I felt the need to compile a short treatise explaining the manner in which Allāh and His Messenger (ﷺ) described how Muslims could increase their money.[2] The

---

[2] For this section, I benefited greatly from Dr. Faḍl Elahi's tract *Mafātīḥ al-Rizq (The Keys to Provision)*, in which he outlined ten ways to increase one's sustenance. I also benefited from Jalāl al-Dīn al-Suyūṭi's (d. 911) tract on this topic, which he entitled, *Uṣūl al-Rifq fi al-Ḥuṣūl ʿala al-Rizq* (published as an article in *Majallah al-Ḥikmah*, v. 3, Muḥarram 1415 A.H., pps. 249-269).

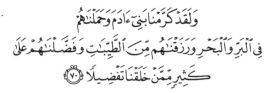

focus of this book is upon encouraging Muslims to procure money through *ḥalāl* means, and to abstain from *ḥarām* gains. Hence, discussion is offered of the fact that wealth, like all elements of the *dunya*, can be either a curse or a blessing, according to how a person obtains and uses it. Furthermore, for those who appreciate that the life of this world and that of the next form a continuum of which worldly existence is only a tiny, virtually insignificant fraction, a reminder is offered on how to accumulate the true currency of success, meaning that which will benefit a person the most in the totality of existence.

The Prophet (ﷺ) predicted,

> "A time will come in which a person will not care whether what he (earned) was through *ḥalāl* or through *ḥarām*."[3]

For those of the audience who do care to have their earnings upon the *ḥalāl*, the following treatise discusses how to maximize a person's earnings thereby. For those who may benefit from the reminder, the true purpose of wealth, its blessings, and the importance of gaining earnings through permissible means are discussed, as are the dreadful consequences of gaining earnings through impermissible means. With that in mind, this book begins with a necessary discussion of the importance of attaining wealth correctly, prior to discussion of how to gain wealth in the first place. For ill-gotten gains may purchase a few transient enjoyments for the brief period of this worldly life, but only correctly gotten gains will have any lasting benefit.

I encourage the readers, if they have any suggestions or come across any mistakes, to share them with me, for indeed the believer is strengthened by the help of others. All comments may be sent care of the publisher.

---

[3] Reported by al-Bukhārī (4/296) and others. See *al-Mishkāt*, (# 2761).

I would like to take this opportunity to express my thanks to my wife Umm Ammaar. She has always been a constant source of motivation throughout the wonderful years that we have been together. Without her patience, dedication and encouragement, this book may never have been written.

Finally, true success is with Allāh alone.

Abu Ammaar

Al-Madīnah al-Nabawiyyah - The City of the Prophet (ﷺ)

16th Dhul-Qa'dah, 1422 A.H.; 30th January, 2002 C.E.

بِسْمِ ٱللَّهِ ٱلرَّحْمَٰنِ ٱلرَّحِيمِ

Wealth: An Introduction

Allāh created man for the sole purpose of worshipping Him. As He said,

وَمَا
خَلَقْتُ ٱلْجِنَّ وَٱلْإِنسَ إِلَّا لِيَعْبُدُونِ ﴿٥٦﴾ مَآ أُرِيدُ مِنْهُم مِّن رِّزْقٍ
وَمَآ أُرِيدُ أَن يُطْعِمُونِ ﴿٥٧﴾ إِنَّ ٱللَّهَ هُوَ ٱلرَّزَّاقُ ذُو ٱلْقُوَّةِ ٱلْمَتِينُ

"And I have not created man and *jinn* (for any other purpose) except to worship Me. I do not need any *rizq* (sustenance) from them, nor do I want that they should feed Me! Verily, Allāh is the only One who is *al-Razzāq* (the Giver and Provider of all Wealth and Sustenance), the Owner of Power, the Most Strong!" [Sūrah *al-Dhāriyāt*, 56-58]

In another verse, the Prophet (ﷺ) was told,

فَٱصْبِرْ عَلَىٰ
مَا يَقُولُونَ وَسَبِّحْ بِحَمْدِ رَبِّكَ قَبْلَ طُلُوعِ ٱلشَّمْسِ وَقَبْلَ غُرُوبِهَا
وَمِنْ ءَانَآئِ ٱلَّيْلِ فَسَبِّحْ وَأَطْرَافَ ٱلنَّهَارِ لَعَلَّكَ تَرْضَىٰ ﴿١٣٠﴾ وَلَا
تَمُدَّنَّ عَيْنَيْكَ إِلَىٰ مَا مَتَّعْنَا بِهِۦٓ أَزْوَٰجًا مِّنْهُمْ زَهْرَةَ ٱلْحَيَوٰةِ ٱلدُّنْيَا
لِنَفْتِنَهُمْ فِيهِ ۚ وَرِزْقُ رَبِّكَ خَيْرٌ وَأَبْقَىٰ ﴿١٣١﴾ وَأْمُرْ أَهْلَكَ بِٱلصَّلَوٰةِ
وَٱصْطَبِرْ عَلَيْهَا ۖ لَا نَسْـَٔلُكَ رِزْقًا ۖ نَّحْنُ نَرْزُقُكَ ۗ وَٱلْعَٰقِبَةُ لِلتَّقْوَىٰ

"So bear patiently what they say, and glorify the praises of your Lord before the rising of the sun, and before its setting ... ...We do not ask you for provision (i.e., to give Us something); (rather) We provide it for you. And the good end (i.e., Paradise) is for those that are conscious (of Allāh)." [Sūrah *Ṭā Hā*, 130-132]

In these verses, Allāh informs us that the purpose of life is to worship Allāh, and Allāh alone. Also, He reminds us that He is not in need of provision (*rizq*) from His creation – rather, He is the One Who supplies a determined provision (*rizq*), thereby providing for the needs of mankind. We find herein an indication that the One Who provides wealth does so for a purpose, and that purpose is to aid us in worshipping Him. In both of the above verses, Allāh combines mention of the concept of worship with assurance of provision from Himself. Thus, the following can be deduced:

- The purpose of creation is to worship Allāh.
- One of the primary distractions from the obligation of worship is the seeking of sustenance. Many of mankind falsely assume that compromising acts of worship so as to increase efforts in seeking earnings will increase a person's wealth (*rizq*).
- Therefore, Allāh assures mankind of their *rizq*, and promises that if they are faithful to Allāh and worship Him alone, He will provide their sustenance and wealth with ease and blessings.
- Allāh does not, however, benefit in any way from mankind — either from our wealth or from our actions. Rather, it is mankind that benefits from the generosity of Allāh, whereas Allāh does not profit in the slightest from His creation.

Wealth, along with all other blessings, is from Allāh. This is mentioned clearly in the Qur'ān, and the two above-quoted verses proclaim this fact. In another verse, Allāh comforts the believers,

وَإِنْ خِفْتُمْ عَيْلَةً فَسَوْفَ يُغْنِيكُمُ ٱللَّهُ مِن فَضْلِهِۦٓ إِن
شَآءَ إِنَّ ٱللَّهَ عَلِيمٌ حَكِيمٌ ﴿٢٨﴾

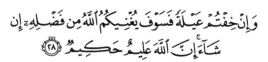

"... and if you fear poverty, then Allāh will enrich you, if He wills, out of His Bounty. Surely, Allāh is All-Knowing, All-Wise." [Sūrah *al-Tawbah*, 28]

Allāh is described in one prayer in the Qur'ān as:

وَتَرۡزُقُ مَن تَشَآءُ بِغَيۡرِ حِسَابٖ

"... and You give wealth (and sustenance) to whom You will, without limit." [Sūrah *Āl-ʿImrān*, 27]

Indeed,

ٱللَّهُ لَطِيفُۢ بِعِبَادِهِۦ يَرۡزُقُ مَن يَشَآءُۖ وَهُوَ ٱلۡقَوِيُّ ٱلۡعَزِيزُ

"Allāh is very Gracious and Kind to His slaves. He gives provisions to whom He wills. And He is the All-Strong, the All-Mighty." [Sūrah *al-Shūra*, 19]

The faithful and wise will recall the source of their sustenance (*rizq*), as Allāh commands,

يَٰٓأَيُّهَا ٱلنَّاسُ ٱذۡكُرُواْ نِعۡمَتَ ٱللَّهِ عَلَيۡكُمۡۚ هَلۡ مِنۡ خَٰلِقٍ غَيۡرُ ٱللَّهِ يَرۡزُقُكُم
مِّنَ ٱلسَّمَآءِ وَٱلۡأَرۡضِۚ

"O Mankind! Remember the Grace of Allāh upon you! Is there any creator other than Allāh who provides for you from the sky and the earth?" [Sūrah *Fāṭir*, 3]

So all creatures, great or small, rely upon Allāh for their *rizq*:

۞ وَمَا مِن دَآبَّةٖ فِي ٱلۡأَرۡضِ إِلَّا عَلَى ٱللَّهِ رِزۡقُهَا وَيَعۡلَمُ مُسۡتَقَرَّهَا
وَمُسۡتَوۡدَعَهَاۚ كُلّٞ فِي كِتَٰبٖ مُّبِينٖ ٦

"And there is no living creature on earth except that its provision (*rizq*) is upon Allāh, and He knows its dwelling place and its resting place. All is in a Clear Book (i.e., *Al-Lawḥ-Al Maḥfūẓ*)." [Sūrah *Hūd*, 6]

Not only is the *rizq* that a person will earn written on the *Lawḥ al-Maḥfūẓ*,[4] it is also written when a person is in the womb of his or her mother. The Prophet (ﷺ) stated, while describing the process of conception,

> "...then the angel comes to it (the embryo), and writes down the length of his life, his deeds, (the amount) of his sustenance, and whether he will be wretched or happy (in the Hereafter)."[5]

So all of a person's wealth has been pre-destined for him (or her) before even being born. No matter what he or she does, it will not be possible to increase or decrease this amount – that which has been pre-destined will come, that which has not, will not.

The Blessings of Wealth

In many verses in the Qur'ān, Allāh commands the believers to enjoy the material blessings which He has provided for them. Allāh states:

كُلُوا۟ وَٱشْرَبُوا۟ مِن رِّزْقِ ٱللَّهِ وَلَا تَعْثَوْا۟ فِى ٱلْأَرْضِ مُفْسِدِينَ

> "Eat and drink of that which Allāh has provided and do not act corruptly, making mischief on the earth." [Sūrah *al-Baqarah*, 60]

Allāh reminds mankind that He is the One Who provides them with their every need:

وَٱذْكُرُوٓا۟ إِذْ أَنتُمْ قَلِيلٌ مُّسْتَضْعَفُونَ فِى ٱلْأَرْضِ تَخَافُونَ
أَن يَتَخَطَّفَكُمُ ٱلنَّاسُ فَـَٔاوَىٰكُمْ وَأَيَّدَكُم بِنَصْرِهِۦ وَرَزَقَكُم
مِّنَ ٱلطَّيِّبَٰتِ لَعَلَّكُمْ تَشْكُرُونَ ﴿٢٦﴾

---

[4] The *Lawḥ al-Maḥfūẓ* is a Tablet in which Allāh has written all that will occur from the time of creation until the Day of Judgement.

[5] Reported by al-Bukhārī (6/303) and others.

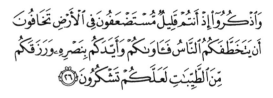

"And remember when you were few and were reckoned weak in the land, and were afraid that men might kidnap you, but He provided a safe place for you, strengthened you with His Help, and provided you with good things so that you might be grateful." [Sūrah *al-Anfāl*, 26]

Allāh states that it is He,

ٱلَّذِى جَعَلَ لَكُمُ
ٱلْأَرْضَ فِرَٰشًا وَٱلسَّمَآءَ بِنَآءً وَأَنزَلَ مِنَ ٱلسَّمَآءِ مَآءً فَأَخْرَجَ
بِهِۦ مِنَ ٱلثَّمَرَٰتِ رِزْقًا لَّكُمْ ۖ فَلَا تَجْعَلُوا۟ لِلَّهِ أَندَادًا وَأَنتُمْ
تَعْلَمُونَ ﴿٢٢﴾

"...who has made the earth a resting place for you, and the sky as a canopy, and sent down rain from the sky and brought forth therewith fruits as a provision for you. Then do not set up rivals unto Allāh (in worship) while you know (that He alone has the right to be worshipped)." [Sūrah *al-Baqarah*, 22]

If a person recognises this, then he should worship only Allāh:

يَٰٓأَيُّهَا ٱلَّذِينَ ءَامَنُوا۟ كُلُوا۟ مِن طَيِّبَٰتِ مَا رَزَقْنَٰكُمْ
وَٱشْكُرُوا۟ لِلَّهِ إِن كُنتُمْ إِيَّاهُ تَعْبُدُونَ ﴿١٧٢﴾

"O you who believe! Eat of the lawful things that We have provided you with, and be grateful to Allāh, if it is indeed He Whom you worship." [Sūrah *al-Baqarah*, 172]

So mankind is commanded to eat, drink and earn their sustenance from the pure and lawful means that Allāh has placed at their disposal. In the end, the blessings that we enjoy, being from Allāh, should incline us to gratitude, and inspire the faithful to greater heights in sincerity and in worship.

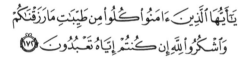

The fact that Allāh has blessed mankind with wealth is yet another indication that man has been given a preferred status over other creations of Allāh:

وَلَقَدْ كَرَّمْنَا بَنِيٓ ءَادَمَ وَحَمَلْنَٰهُمْ
فِي ٱلْبَرِّ وَٱلْبَحْرِ وَرَزَقْنَٰهُم مِّنَ ٱلطَّيِّبَٰتِ وَفَضَّلْنَٰهُمْ عَلَىٰ
كَثِيرٖ مِّمَّنْ خَلَقْنَا تَفْضِيلٗا ﴿٧٠﴾

> "And We have certainly honoured the Children of Ādam, and carried them on the land and sea, and provided for them of the good things, and preferred them over much of what We have created, with [definite] preference." [Sūrah *al-Isrā*, 70]

In another verse, Allāh commands those who are entrusted with the property of orphans to control and protect such wealth until the orphans reach maturity, and become capable of caring for it themselves with responsibility:

وَلَا تُؤْتُواْ ٱلسُّفَهَآءَ أَمْوَٰلَكُمُ ٱلَّتِي جَعَلَ ٱللَّهُ لَكُمْ قِيَٰمٗا

> "And do not give the weak-minded (i.e., young orphans) your property, which Allāh has made a means of sustenance for you." [Sūrah *al-Nisā*, 5]

Note that this property is referred to as 'your property', even though the reference is to the orphans' property, thus signifying the collective obligation of preserving and protecting wealth.

Ibn al-Jawzī writes,

> As for the nobility of money, then verily Allāh has praised its status, and commanded us to protect it… And Saʿīd ibn al-Musayyib said, 'There is no good in a person who does not seek money; with it, he can protect his honour, and be gracious to his relatives, and, were he to die, he would leave it for his inheritors.' And when he (i.e., Saʿīd) died, he left behind four hundred gold coins. And Sufyān al-Thawrī left behind two hundred, and he is the one who said, 'Money in our times is like a weapon.'

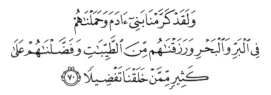

The early generations continued to praise money, and save it in order to use at times of emergency. They would help the poor with it. However, some of them avoided it in order to prevent themselves from being distracted from worship, and in order to concentrate (on their worship). So they used to be satisfied with small amounts. And if someone were to say: It is better to have less of it, then he would be close to the truth.[6]

The Desirability of Obtaining Money

It is not a sin for a person to wish for more money, as long as his or her intentions are pure. Once the Prophet (ﷺ) called for ʿAmr ibn al-ʿĀṣ, and ordered him to bring his armour and weapons. When he arrived, the Prophet (ﷺ) looked at him and said,

> "I wish to send you out on an expedition in which you will gain plenty of booty, and you will come back safely, and I wish that you come back with a good amount of money (because of the booty)."

ʿAmr replied, "O Messenger of Allāh! I did not accept Islām in order to increase my wealth! Rather, I accepted it out of a sincere desire for Islām!" To which the Prophet (ﷺ) replied,

> "O ʿAmr! How admirable is pure money for a righteous person!"[7]

He (ﷺ) also said,

> "There is no harm in richness, for he who has *taqwa*, but good health is better than being rich, for he who has *taqwa*."[8]

---

[6] Paraphrased from *Talbīs Iblīs*, pps. 231-234.

[7] Reported by al-Ḥākim (2/3) with this story, and he authenticated it, and al-Dhahabī agreed with him, and Aḥmad (5/272). Al-Albānī agreed with them and considered it authentic in his *al-Silsilah al-Ṣaḥīḥah* (# 174).

[8] Reported by Ibn Mājah (# 2141), and al-Būṣayrī said, "Its *isnād* is authentic," as did al-Albānī in *Silsilah al-Ṣaḥīḥah* (# 174).

So there is no harm in seeking money and desiring it, as long as the means to achieve it, and the intention for which it is desired, is permissible. Wealth is essential for a person to survive in this life, and, if possessed in excess of one's needs, can be used in such a manner as to incur the pleasure of Allāh. It is for this reason that the Prophet (ﷺ) stated that it is a noble possession, but only for a righteous person, for only the pious person will use wealth properly, unhindered by the selfishness which deprives wealth of so many blessings.

The Prophet (ﷺ) stated,

> "This money is green and luscious (like ripe fruits), so he who takes it rightfully, then what a great aid it is for him!"[9]

In this ḥadīth we are told the true purpose of money, and that it can be a tool that helps us to worship Allāh. So in this is a great blessing, for everything that assists in the worship of Allāh helps the faithful to achieve their goal of paradise. Therefore, to seek, spend, and protect money can all be acts of worship, if done with correctness and purity of intention.

For this reason, the Prophet (ﷺ) used to ask Allāh to bless him with sufficient sustenance, and seek refuge in Allāh from poverty. He would regularly supplicate after the prayer,

> "O Allāh! I ask you for beneficial knowledge, and a good sustenance (*rizq*), and deeds that are accepted (by you)."[10]

He (ﷺ) would also supplicate, three times at sunrise and three times at sunset,

---

[9] Reported with this wording by Ibn Abī al-Dunyā in *Iṣlāḥ al-Māl* (# 3), and with various other wordings by Muslim (# 6883), al-Tirmidhī (3/277) and others.

[10] Reported by Ibn Mājah (# 925); al-Būṣayrī stated that its narrators were trustworthy, and al-Albānī considered it authentic in his *Ṣaḥīḥ Ibn Mājah* (1/152).

> "O Allāh! I seek your refuge from disbelief (*kufr*) and poverty, and I seek your refuge from the punishment of the grave. There is no deity worthy of worship except you."[11]

Lastly, he would close the day by making the following *du'ā* before going to sleep,

> "...O Allāh! Pay off my debts, and make us rich from poverty."[12]

The Prophet Muḥammad (ﷺ) commanded the Muslims to do likewise. 'Ubādah ibn al-Ṣāmit related that the Prophet (ﷺ) said,

> "Seek refuge in Allāh from poverty, and destitution, and that someone wrongs you or you wrong others."[13]

He would also teach any person who had accepted Islām to make the following supplication following every prayer,

> "O Allāh! Forgive me, and have mercy on me. Guide me, and give me health, and good sustenance."[14]

Once, the mother of his servant Anas came to him (ﷺ), and asked him, "O Messenger of Allāh! Your little servant Anas – pray for him." So he (ﷺ) prayed,

> "O Allāh! Increase his money and children, and bless him in whatever you give him."

Many years later, Anas said, "There is no one from the Anṣār who has more money that I do, and my daughter Umaynah informed me that when Ḥajjāj attacked Baṣra (and killed many of

---

[11] Reported by Abū Dāwūd (4/324), Aḥmad (5/42), and others. Ibn Bāz considered it to be *ḥasan* in *Tuḥfat al-Akhyār*, p. 26.

[12] Reported by Muslim (4/2084) and others.

[13] Reported by al-Ṭabarānī in his *al-Kabīr*. Although al-Haythamī pointed out that its chain is slightly weak (in his *Majma' al-Zawā'id*, 10/143), there is supporting evidence for it in other narrations, so the ḥadīth is authentic, as al-Albānī mentions in his *al-Ṣaḥīḥah* (# 1445)

[14] Reported by Muslim (4/2073) and others.

its inhabitants) over one hundred and twenty of my offspring were amongst those buried."[15]

In order to demonstrate the permissibility of desiring more wealth, the Prophet (ﷺ) narrated,

> "Once, while (the Prophet) Ayūb was taking a bath naked, locusts of gold fell upon him. So he started to gather them in his clothes. His Lord called out to him, 'O Ayūb! Have I not given you riches?' He replied, 'Yes, indeed, my Lord, but I can never be self-sufficient from your blessings!'"

In another narration, he responded,

> "...but who is there that can be satisfied with your Mercy (so that he does not desire more)?"[16]

Al-Ḥāfiẓ Ibn Ḥajr states, commenting on this ḥadīth, "In this ḥadīth, the permissibility of being eager to increase one's (money) through *ḥalāl* means is shown, but this is for the one who is confident that he will be able to thank Allāh (with the money once he obtains it). Another point of benefit is that money that is achieved through lawful (i.e., *ḥalāl*) means has been called 'blessings' (*barakah*). Furthermore, this ḥadīth shows the superiority of the rich man who is thankful."[17]

In the above ḥadīth we find the Prophet of Allāh, Ayūb (Job), the patient one, so eager to collect the wealth and blessings of Allāh that he uses the very clothes with which he covers his nakedness to collect the treasure. And when Allāh, though being All-Knowing and All-Aware of His servants, questions him about his eagerness, Ayūb responds that no one can be satisfied with any amount of blessings from Allāh, for he will always want more and more.

---

[15] Reported by al-Bukhārī (# 202) and others.

[16] Reported by al-Bukhārī (# 3391), al-Nasā'ī (# 407) and others.

[17] *Fatḥ al-Bārī*, v. 6, p. 485.

The Purpose of Money

So great is the status and blessing of wealth, that mankind judges one another on this basis. Monetary wealth is the primary factor in determining social status, for in its presence power and fame increase, whereas in its absence power and fame are lost.

For this reason, the Prophet (ﷺ) stated, "Status (*ḥasab*) is (based) on money." This does not, of course, imply that a person of wealth is better than one who lacks wealth. Rather, the Prophet (ﷺ) merely narrated the *status quo* of mankind – that people judge one another based on their financial status. This is clearly seen in another wording of this ḥadīth, in which the Prophet Muḥammad (ﷺ) said,

> "Indeed, the status of the people of this world that they go to (i.e., judge by) is money."

However, in yet another narration, he (ﷺ) concluded this ḥadīth by stating that

> "...the true nobility is *taqwa*."[18]

Although the actual *purpose* of wealth is not the attainment of status, we nonetheless find that this is one of the main by-products of wealth. Perhaps the most explicit ḥadīth that mentions the purpose of money is that of Abū Wāqid al-Laythī, who relates: "We used to go to the Prophet (ﷺ) whenever some (Qur'ān) was revealed, so he would recite it to us. One day, he said,

---

[18] Reported by al-Tirmidhī (2/222) who considered it *ḥasan ṣaḥīḥ gharīb*; Ibn Mājah (# 4219) (and al-Būṣayrī pointed out that its chain is weak); Aḥmad (5/361); al-Ḥākim (2/163) who considered it *Ṣaḥīḥ* and al-Dhahabī agreed with him; Ibn Ḥibbān (# 699 and 700 – Ibn Bilibban's editing) and others. Al-Būṣayrī is correct that the chain of Ibn Mājah is weak; however, the ḥadīth is reported with another chain in the other books, and therefore al-Tirmidhī's verdict that it is *ḥasan* is correct, and this is the opinion of Shu'ayb al-Arna'ūṭ and al-Albānī (see *Irwā al-Ghalīl*, # 1870 and 1871).

'Allāh has said: I have sent down money so that the prayer can be established, and *zakāt* be given. And if the son of Ādam had a valley (in one narration: a valley of gold), he would still wish for another, and if he had two valleys (in one narration: two valleys of gold), he would wish for a third! And nothing will fill the inside of the son of Ādam except dust, and Allāh will accept the repentance of he who repents."[19]

So money has been revealed to be a natural, innate lust of mankind, and for this reason serves to test the sincerity of faith on the part of those who are blessed with wealth. Those who are successful in the religion will turn to Allāh in prayer and sacrifice, spending of their time and energy in prayer as commanded, and of their wealth as prescribed according to the rules of *zakāt*. Wealth is a necessary commodity for us in our long journey of the worship of Allāh. Without money, we would not be able to arrive at our final destination of the Pleasure of Allāh.

In numerous verses, Allāh mentions the blessings of those who pray, and in many others, of those who spend their money for His sake. It is significant to note that Allāh frequently mentions the *zakāt* in the same verses as *ṣalāt*, thus indicating the importance of spending money for His sake. In one verse, He mentions spending money as the primary cause for being saved from the Fire of Hell:

وَسَيُجَنَّبُهَا ٱلْأَتْقَى ﴿١٧﴾ ٱلَّذِى يُؤْتِى مَالَهُۥ يَتَزَكَّىٰ ﴿١٨﴾

"And the pious (person) will be far removed from it (Hell); he who spends his wealth in order to purify himself." [Sūrah *al-Layl*, 17-18]

In conclusion, the Prophet (ﷺ) has divided all people into four categories in regard to wealth. The Prophet (ﷺ) stated,

---

[19] Reported by Aḥmad (5/218) and al-Ṭabarānī in his *al-Kabīr* (# 3301) with an authentic chain, as mentioned in *al-Ṣaḥīḥah*, (# 1639).

> "Three matters, I will swear about them (that they are truthful) and I will narrate to you something, so memorize it. (The three matters are:) Money will never decrease because of charity, and no person was ever wronged, and he was patient, except that Allāh will add to his honour, and no person opened for himself the door of asking (others for money), except that Allāh will open for him a door of poverty. And I will narrate to you this, so memorize it: This world has only four types of people (in it). (The first) is a person whom Allāh has blessed with money and knowledge, so he fears Allāh with regards to it, and he uses it to support his relatives, and he gives Allāh's rights on it. So this person is the highest in rank. (The second) is a person whom Allāh has blessed with knowledge, but he does not have money. So he has a sincere intention. He says, 'If only I had money, I would do as so-and-so does (the first person).' He will be (rewarded) for his intention, and his reward is the same (as the first person's). (The third) is a person whom Allāh gave money, but did not give any knowledge. So he is involved in his money without any knowledge (i.e., gaining it through *ḥarām* and spending it on *ḥarām*). He does not fear his Lord regarding it, nor does he fulfil the ties of kinship with it. He does not know the rights of Allāh upon it. So this person is at the filthiest status. (The fourth) is a person whom Allāh gave neither money nor knowledge. He says, 'If only I had money, I would do like so-and-so (the third person) does.' He will be (punished) for his intention, and his sin is the same (as the third person's)."[20]

Of the above-mentioned four categories of people, the first and second are those Muslims who wish to spend their money for the sake of Allāh. These are those who wish to use the blessings of Allāh to obtain His pleasure, and by this path they obtain even

---

[20] Reported by al-Tirmidhī (# 2325), who said it was *ḥasan ṣaḥīḥ*, and Aḥmad (4/231). Al-Albānī agreed with al-Tirmidhī's verdict in his *Ṣaḥīḥ al-Targhīb, (#* 14).

more blessings thereby. However, the people of the second category do not possess the money to fulfil their desired goals, in contrast to those of the first category. But due to the great mercy of Allāh, both types of people will be rewarded equally, the first because of their actions, the second because of their sincere intentions. People of the third and fourth categories are those whose actions or intentions are to spend in the path of worldly desires, careless of the rights of Allāh upon their wealth. Hence, they do not care how they earn their money (whether by *ḥalāl* or by *ḥarām*), nor do they concern themselves with Allāh's restrictions upon its use. To them, money is nothing more than a tool by which to satisfy their bodily desires. The third category actually has the money to accomplish this ignoble goal, whereas the fourth category merely envies the third for their ability to do so.

An important point needs to be stressed in this regard, for Allāh does not forbid the spending of wealth in the fulfillment of desires. Rather, Allāh restricts the gaining of wealth to lawful means, the expenditure upon lawful enjoyments, and further, Allāh defines His rights (such as that of *zakāt*) upon wealth. An essential difference between the first two categories of people, described in the above *ḥadīth*, and the second two categories, is not in the actual *enjoyment* of wealth. Rather, the difference is between the lawful and unlawful attainment of wealth, the lawful and unlawful spending thereof, and recognizing versus denying the rights of Allāh upon that wealth, whether actually possessed or simply desired. So, in the infinite wisdom of Allāh, just as both of the first two categories deserve reward, the first for actions and the second for intention, so too are the third and fourth categories deserving of equal punishment, the one for evil action, the other for equally evil and ignorant intention.

The *Fitnah* of Wealth

Wealth, while one of the greatest blessings that mankind has been given, is at the same time one of the greatest trials and temptations. Allāh states,

إِنَّمَآ أَمۡوَٰلُكُمۡ وَأَوۡلَٰدُكُمۡ فِتۡنَةٞۚ وَٱللَّهُ عِندَهُۥٓ أَجۡرٌ عَظِيمٞ ﴿١٥﴾

"Your wealth and your children are only a trial (*fitnah*). And Allāh - With Him is a great reward (Paradise)." [Sūrah *al-Taghābun*, 15]

He also states,

وَٱعۡلَمُوٓاْ أَنَّمَآ أَمۡوَٰلُكُمۡ وَأَوۡلَٰدُكُمۡ فِتۡنَةٞ وَأَنَّ ٱللَّهَ
عِندَهُۥٓ أَجۡرٌ عَظِيمٞ ﴿٢٨﴾

"And know that your possessions and your children are but a trial (*fitnah*) and that surely with Allāh is a mighty reward." [Sūrah *al-Anfāl*, 28]

Hence, every material possession is only a test and a trial. To make this test even more difficult, the value of wealth is raised high above most other worldly goods. Almost every person has a strong craving for wealth. As Allāh says,

زُيِّنَ لِلنَّاسِ حُبُّ ٱلشَّهَوَٰتِ مِنَ ٱلنِّسَآءِ
وَٱلۡبَنِينَ وَٱلۡقَنَٰطِيرِ ٱلۡمُقَنطَرَةِ مِنَ ٱلذَّهَبِ وَٱلۡفِضَّةِ
وَٱلۡخَيۡلِ ٱلۡمُسَوَّمَةِ وَٱلۡأَنۡعَٰمِ وَٱلۡحَرۡثِۗ ذَٰلِكَ مَتَٰعُ
ٱلۡحَيَوٰةِ ٱلدُّنۡيَاۖ وَٱللَّهُ عِندَهُۥ حُسۡنُ ٱلۡمَـَٔابِ ﴿١٤﴾

"Beautified for men is the love of things they covet; women, children, much of gold and silver (wealth), branded beautiful horses, cattle and well-tilled land. This is the pleasure of the present world's life; but Allāh has the excellent return (Paradise) with Him." [Sūrah *Āl-ʿImrān*, 14]

In one of the most explicit verses in this regard in the Qur'ān, the Muslim is advised to understand his priorities, or suffer the consequences:

قُلْ إِن كَانَ ءَابَآؤُكُمْ وَأَبْنَآؤُكُمْ وَإِخْوَٰنُكُمْ وَأَزْوَٰجُكُمْ وَعَشِيرَتُكُمْ وَأَمْوَٰلٌ ٱقْتَرَفْتُمُوهَا وَتِجَٰرَةٌ تَخْشَوْنَ كَسَادَهَا وَمَسَٰكِنُ تَرْضَوْنَهَآ أَحَبَّ إِلَيْكُم مِّنَ ٱللَّهِ وَرَسُولِهِۦ وَجِهَادٍ فِى سَبِيلِهِۦ فَتَرَبَّصُوا۟ حَتَّىٰ يَأْتِىَ ٱللَّهُ بِأَمْرِهِۦ ۗ وَٱللَّهُ لَا يَهْدِى ٱلْقَوْمَ ٱلْفَٰسِقِينَ ﴿٢٤﴾

"Say: If your fathers, your sons, your brothers, your wives, your kindred, the wealth that you have gained, the commerce in which you fear a decline, and the dwellings in which you delight, are more beloved to you than Allāh and His Messenger, and striving in His Cause, then wait until Allāh executes His Decision (torment). And Allāh guides not the people who are rebellious (disobedient to Allāh)." [Sūrah *al-Tawbah*, 24]

Countless verses censure those who hoard wealth in denial of Allāh's rights:

وَيْلٌ لِّكُلِّ هُمَزَةٍ لُّمَزَةٍ ﴿١﴾ ٱلَّذِى جَمَعَ مَالًا وَعَدَّدَهُۥ ﴿٢﴾ يَحْسَبُ أَنَّ مَالَهُۥٓ أَخْلَدَهُۥ ﴿٣﴾

"Woe to every slanderer and backbiter. Who has gathered wealth and counted it. He presumes that his money will make him immortal." [Sūrah *al-Humazah*, 1-3]

And:

أَفَرَءَيْتَ ٱلَّذِى كَفَرَ بِـَٔايَٰتِنَا وَقَالَ لَأُوتَيَنَّ مَالًا وَوَلَدًا

"Have you seen him who disbelieved in Our verses and (yet) says: 'I shall certainly be given wealth and children.'" [Sūrah *Maryam*, 77]

Allāh threatens such people:

ذَرۡنِي وَمَنۡ خَلَقۡتُ وَحِيدٗا ﴿١١﴾ وَجَعَلۡتُ لَهُۥ مَالٗا مَّمۡدُودٗا ﴿١٢﴾ وَبَنِينَ شُهُودٗا ﴿١٣﴾ وَمَهَّدتُّ لَهُۥ تَمۡهِيدٗا ﴿١٤﴾ ثُمَّ يَطۡمَعُ أَنۡ أَزِيدَ ﴿١٥﴾

"Leave Me Alone [to deal] with whom I created alone [without any wealth or children]! And then granted extensive wealth. And children present [with him]. And spread [everything] before him, easing [his life]. Then, he desires that I should add [yet] more!" [Sūrah *al-Mudathir*, 11-15]

As for such people,

مَآ أَغۡنَىٰ عَنۡهُ مَالُهُۥ وَمَا كَسَبَ ﴿٢﴾

" His wealth will not benefit him, nor that which he gained [in this life]!"[Sūrah *al-Masad*, 2]

In fact, the very money that they are supposedly 'blessed' with is a means of punishment for them. Allāh states, comforting the Prophet (ﷺ),

فَلَا تُعۡجِبۡكَ أَمۡوَٰلُهُمۡ وَلَآ أَوۡلَٰدُهُمۡۚ إِنَّمَا يُرِيدُ ٱللَّهُ لِيُعَذِّبَهُم بِهَا فِي ٱلۡحَيَوٰةِ ٱلدُّنۡيَا وَتَزۡهَقَ أَنفُسُهُمۡ وَهُمۡ كَٰفِرُونَ ﴿٥٥﴾

"So let not their wealth or their children amaze you (O Muḥammad); in reality Allāh's Plan is to punish them with these things in the life of this world, and that their souls shall depart (die) while they are disbelievers." [Sūrah *al-Tawbah*, 55]

In yet another verse,

وَلَا يَحۡسَبَنَّ ٱلَّذِينَ كَفَرُوٓاْ أَنَّمَا نُمۡلِي لَهُمۡ خَيۡرٞ لِّأَنفُسِهِمۡۚ إِنَّمَا نُمۡلِي لَهُمۡ لِيَزۡدَادُوٓاْ إِثۡمٗاۚ وَلَهُمۡ عَذَابٞ مُّهِينٞ ﴿١٧٨﴾

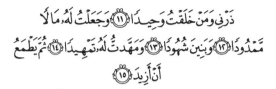

> “And let not those who disbelieve ever think that [because] We extend their time [of enjoyment] it is better for them. We only extend it for them so that they may increase in sin, and for them is a humiliating punishment.” [Sūrah *Āl-ʿImran*, 178]

By these verses, we come to understand that an unrighteous life of wealth and worldly enjoyments is not a blessing, but rather a curse.

In truth, man is tested both in wealth and in poverty:

فَأَمَّا
الْإِنسَانُ إِذَا مَا ابْتَلَاهُ رَبُّهُ فَأَكْرَمَهُ وَنَعَّمَهُ فَيَقُولُ رَبِّي أَكْرَمَنِ
﴿١٥﴾ وَأَمَّا إِذَا مَا ابْتَلَاهُ فَقَدَرَ عَلَيْهِ رِزْقَهُ فَيَقُولُ رَبِّي أَهَانَنِ ﴿١٦﴾
كَلَّا بَل لَّا تُكْرِمُونَ الْيَتِيمَ ﴿١٧﴾ وَلَا تَحَاضُّونَ عَلَىٰ طَعَامِ
الْمِسْكِينِ ﴿١٨﴾ وَتَأْكُلُونَ التُّرَاثَ أَكْلًا لَّمًّا ﴿١٩﴾
وَتُحِبُّونَ الْمَالَ حُبًّا جَمًّا ﴿٢٠﴾

> “As for man, when his Lord tries him by giving him honour and gifts, then he says (puffed up): ‘My Lord has honoured me.’ But when He tries him, by straitening his means of life, he says: ‘My Lord has humiliated me!’ Nay! But you treat not the orphans with kindness or generosity! And urge not on the feeding of the poor! And devour inheritance - all with greed! And you love wealth with a great love!” [Sūrah *al-Fajr*, 15-20]

So great is the *fitnah* of wealth that this was the main fear that the Prophet (ﷺ) expressed for his nation. He stated,

> “I don’t fear poverty for you, but rather I fear that you will compete with one another (to see who has more possessions).”[21]

---

[21] Reported by al-Ḥākim (2/543) and others. Al-Ḥākim stated that it was authentic, and al-Dhahabi agreed with him, as did al-Albānī in *Ṣaḥīḥ al-Jāmiʿ* (# 5523).

In describing the evils of greed, he (ﷺ) gave a beautiful parable:

> "Two hungry wolves, if let loose amongst a flock of sheep, cause less harm than a man's eagerness to increase his money and his prestige."[22]

In another ḥadīth, he (ﷺ) stated,

> "Three things destroy, and three things save. As for the three things that destroy, they are: greediness that is obeyed, and desires that are followed, and a person becoming self-conceited (and proud) with himself. As for the three things that save, they are: the fear of Allāh in secret and public, and moderation in poverty and richness, and fairness in anger and pleasure."[23]

Extreme love for this world cannot exist in a heart devoted to Allāh. The Prophet (ﷺ) predicted,

> "The Day of Judgement has come close, and mankind will only increase their desire for this world, and they will only go farther and farther away from Allāh."[24]

There is a direct relationship between a love of this world and loss of devotion to Allāh; the more a person loves this world, the less he loves Allāh, and vice-versa.

Therefore, one's love for money will harm him in this world, and in the Hereafter as well. On the Day of Judgement, every

---

[22] Reported by al-Tirmidhī (# 2373), Aḥmad and others. Al-Tirmidhī considered it authentic, as did al-Albānī in *Ṣaḥīḥ al-Jāmi'* (# 5620).

[23] Reported by al-Bazzār (# 80), Abū Nu'aym in his *Ḥilya* (2/343), al-Bayhaqī in his *Shu'ab al-Īman* (2/382) and others, with various chains. Al-Mundhirī wrote (1/162), "All of these chains, even though none of them is safe from criticism, put together raise the ḥadīth to the level of *ḥasan*, Allāh-willing." And al-Albānī agreed with that (see *al-Ṣaḥīḥah*, # 1802).

[24] Reported by al-Ḥākim (4/324) who declared it to be authentic, and al-Albānī agreed with him (*al-Ṣaḥīḥah,* # 1510).

single person will be questioned about the money that he or she has earned. In fact, this questioning will take place as soon as one is resurrected from the grave. The Prophet (ﷺ) stated,

> "The two feet of the son of Ādam will not move on the Day of Judgement in front of his Lord until he is asked about five things: about his life, and how he spent it? And about his youth, what did he consume it in? And about his money, how did he earn it? And what did he spend it on? And how much did he act upon what he knew?"[25]

Out of these five questions, two deal with money.

For the above reasons, the majority of businessmen and traders will be resurrected amongst the sinful on the Day of Judgement. The Prophet (ﷺ) said,

> "The businessmen will be resurrected on the Day of Judgement amongst the sinful (*fujjār*), except those who have *taqwa* of Allāh, and are honest and truthful."[26]

This ḥadīth shows that dealing with money, in general, leads a person to injustice and sin. The more one is involved with increasing his wealth, the greater the chance that he or she will fall into sin while trying to accrue such wealth. Only the person who truly has the fear of Allāh (*taqwa*) will be able to save himself from such temptation.

As for the poor, they will not have great amounts of money which they will have to account for. For this reason, they will enter Paradise long before the rich; while the rich are standing in front of Allāh, answering for every penny that they earned and spent, the poor will have finished their examination and moved on to their assigned fate. Abū Hurayrah narrated that the Prophet (ﷺ) said,

---

[25] Reported by al-Tirmidhī (2/67) who declared it *ḥasan ṣaḥīḥ*, and others. See *al-Silsilah*, (# 946).

[26] Reported by al-Tirmidhī (1/228) who declared it *ḥasan ṣaḥīḥ*, and al-Ḥākim (2/6) who authenticated it, as did al-Albānī (*al-Ṣaḥīḥah*, # 994).

> "The poor will enter Paradise before the rich by half a day, and that is five hundred years."[27]

A day in the sight of Allāh is like a thousand years, thus half a day is equivalent to five hundred years. So the rich will have to wait this long period of time – a time that is equivalent to more than ten generations – while the poor are enjoying the blessings of Paradise.

It is for all of these reasons that the Prophet (ﷺ) used to pray:

> "O Allāh! I seek your refuge from the evils of the *fitnah* of wealth, and the evils of the *fitnah* of poverty."[28]

Both poverty and wealth are *fitnahs* – ways by which Allāh tries and tests us.

A person cannot remain upon two divergent paths, or retain a tight grip on two items moving in opposite directions. Given that the path to fulfilment of illicit worldly desires and the path to the pleasure of Allāh travel in different directions, excessive love of wealth risks compromising obedience to Allāh, and the blessings to be gained from seeking His pleasure. This section can be summarised in the ḥadīth of the Prophet (ﷺ) in which he said,

> "The plentiful (i.e., the rich) will be the lowest on the Day of Judgement, except he who distributed his money left and right (i.e., at all times), while he earned from pure (means)."[29]

---

[27] Reported by al-Tirmidhī (# 2353) who said it is *ḥasan ṣaḥīḥ*; Ibn Mājah (# 4122); and Aḥmad (2/513); and it is as al-Tirmidhī said.

[28] Reported by al-Bukhārī (11/176) and Muslim (# 2078).

[29] Reported by Ibn Mājah (# 4130), Ibn Ḥibbān (# 807), Aḥmad (2/340), and others, with various similar wordings. Al-Būṣayrī said (2/278), "This is a *Ṣaḥīḥ* chain; its narrators are all trustworthy," and al-Albānī also considered the ḥadīth authentic (*al-Ṣaḥīḥah* # 1766).

The Importance of *Ḥalāl* Sustenance

There is no doubt that one of the obligations upon the Muslim is that he earn for himself and his family a pure and *ḥalāl* sustenance. Abū Hurayrah narrated that the Prophet (ﷺ) said:

> "O People! Allāh is *al-Ṭayyib* (Pure), and He only accepts that which is pure! Allāh has commanded the believers what He has commanded the Messengers, for He said, 'O Messengers! Eat from the pure foods, and do right,' and He said, 'O you who believe! Eat from the pure and good foods We have given you.'"

Then the Prophet (ﷺ) mentioned a traveller on a long journey, who is dishevelled and dusty, and he stretches forth his hands to the sky, saying, "O my Lord! O my Lord!" – while his food is unlawful, his drink is unlawful, his clothing is unlawful, and he is nourished unlawfully; how can he (expect to) be answered?[30] It is noticed in this ḥadīth that the Prophet (ﷺ) emphasised this person's impure earnings by detailing the fact that his food, clothes, drink and nourishment were all obtained from the impure.

From this ḥadīth, we learn that both the prophets and the believers have been commanded to eat from the *ṭayyibāt*, or the pure things. Purity is achieved when one earns his sustenance in a *ḥalāl* manner, and then uses it to buy *ḥalāl* food. So, if a person buys pure food from stolen money, this will not be accepted from him. Likewise, if one earns money from permissible means, then uses it to buy impermissible items, such as intoxicants, this too will not be accepted from him. Only when both of these conditions have been met – the way one earns money and the way one spends it – will Allāh's acceptance be gained.

Another ḥadīth affirms the above:

---

[30] Reported by Aḥmad (2/328), Muslim (2/703), and al-Tirmidhī (5/220) from Abū Hurayrah.

> "Whoever gives charity equivalent to a date, from his pure earnings – and Allāh only accepts pure – then Allāh will accept it with His right hand, then He will nurture it for its companion, like one of you nurtures his foal, until it becomes like a mountain."[31]

So charity that is given from impure earnings will not be accepted by Allāh, no matter how much is given, whereas charity given from pure earnings will be accepted by Allāh, even if equivalent to a date!

Furthermore, there are a number of narrations that signify that earning through *ḥalāl* is an obligation upon every Muslim.[32] It is because of this that Islām encourages working. The taking of a profession is encouraged because it is one of the best ways that a person can ensure earning pure sustenance. ʿUmar ibn al-Khaṭṭāb said, "I see a man that impresses me, so I ask, 'Does he have a profession (through which he earns money)?' So if they say, 'No,' then he falls from my eyes (and I do not respect him)."[33]

So great is the status of *ḥalāl* sustenance that Islām has not looked down upon manual labour. Instead, it has given it a very high place, due to the fact that manual labour is, in general, a very honest profession. The Prophet (ﷺ) stated,

> "No one has ever eaten any food that is better than eating what his hands have earned. And indeed the Prophet of Allāh, Dāwūd, would eat from the earnings of his hands."[34]

---

[31] Reported by al-Bukhārī (# 1410) and others.

[32] There are various wordings of this narration, one of them being, "The seeking of *ḥalāl* sustenance is an obligation upon the Muslim." However, none of these narrations are authentic. Some scholars, such as al-Sakhāwī, consider the ḥadīth to be *ḥasan* due to all of its weak chains (see his *al-Maqāṣid al-Ḥasanah*, # 801), whereas others, such as al-Albānī, hold it to be weak (see *al-Mishkāt,* # 2781). In any case, the meaning of the ḥadīth is without a doubt correct.

[33] *Kanz al-Ummāl*, (4/123).

[34] Reported by al-Bukhārī (2/10) and others.

In this ḥadīth, we are told that the most honourable way to earn money is through manual labour, for even the Prophet Dāwūd would earn his sustenance by making armour and selling it. Furthermore, the Prophet (ﷺ) said,

> "The prophet Zakariyya was a carpenter."[35]

This great Prophet of Allāh, who took care of Maryam the mother of ʿĪsa, used to earn his livelihood through the noble profession of carpentry.

In fact, even the Prophet of Allāh(ﷺ) used to earn from his own hands. Once, he (ﷺ) stated,

> "Allāh did not send any prophet except that he used to be a shepherd of sheep."

So the companions asked, "Including you, O Messenger of Allāh?" He replied,

> "Yes, I used to be a shepherd for the people of Makkah, in return for some *qararīt* (i.e., coins of copper)."[36]

The Prophet (ﷺ) was not embarrassed or ashamed to inform his companions that he used to work as a shepherd in return for a very small amount of money (*qararīṭ*).

As mentioned earlier, there are two aspects to *ḥalāl* sustenance, the first involving earning through *ḥalāl* means (as discussed above), and the second entailing spending only on *ḥalāl* items so as to ensure purity in what a person eats, drinks and is nourished on.

The Prophet (ﷺ) was very cautious in what he ate. He would make sure that every morsel of food was *ḥalāl* for him. He (ﷺ) said,

---

[35] Reported by Muslim (# 2379) and others.

[36] Reported by al-Bukhārī (2/48) and others.

> "I sometimes return home to my family, and I find a date fallen on my bed, so I pick it up to eat it, but then I fear that it might be from charity, so I throw it away."[37]

On another occasion, the Prophet (ﷺ) could not sleep all night, tossing and turning. So his wife asked him, "O Messenger of Allāh! You spent the night awake, tossing and turning?" He replied,

> "I found a date last night under my side, and ate it. (Then I remembered) that we had (in our house) some dates that were meant for charity. So I feared that the date (that I ate) was of it."[38]

Subhān Allāh! The Prophet (ﷺ) ate one date, forgetting that he had some dates in his house that were meant to be distributed to the poor, and this caused him to have a sleepless night for fear that it might have been from the dates of charity! So how is it that this accidental morsel, which a person would hope to have been forgiven on the basis of innocent intention even had it been *ḥarām*, caused our beloved Prophet (ﷺ) so much unrest and discomfort, while one of us might earn his or her entire living through means that are *ḥarām* without a doubt, and yet still enjoy a deep sleep at night?

The Companions, too, were careful about how they earned their sustenance. Once, a servant of Abū Bakr's came to him with some food, so he ate from it. The servant then asked him, "Do you know where this came from?" He replied, "From where?" The servant responded, "I practised astrology once in the times of *Jahiliyyah* – even though I am not an expert in it, except that I

---

[37] Reported by al-Bukhārī (# 232) and Muslim (# 1069). It was not allowed for the Prophet (ﷺ) or his family to eat from charity.

[38] Reported by Aḥmad in his *Musnad* (2/183 and 193), and considered authentic by al-Arnaʿūṭ in his checking of *Sharḥ al-Arbaʿīn* (p. 198).

managed to trick the other person.[39] So he paid me, and gave me what you ate!" Hearing this, Abū Bakr put his finger in his mouth and forced himself to vomit up the food, until there was nothing left in his stomach.[40] A similar incident is reported from ʿUmar ibn al-Khaṭṭāb, when he was given some milk by his servant, and then found out that the milk was from the camels that were meant for charity.[41] In yet another indication of the piety of the early generations, Saʿad ibn Abī Waqās, one of the famous Companions of the Prophet (ﷺ), was once asked, "Why is it that your prayers are responded to, amongst all of the other Companions?" So he replied, "I do not raise to my mouth a morsel except that I know where it came from and where it came out of."[42]

In conclusion, the Prophet (ﷺ) gave an example contrasting the person who takes from this world excessively, not caring how he earns his money, with the person who takes from it moderately, ensuring that his earnings are *ḥalāl*. He (ﷺ) said,

> "What I fear for you after me (is) what will be given to you from the magnificence and beauty of this world, except that good never brings about evil. The fruits that are harvested in spring cause death (for the animal that eats it), or brings it close to death, except for the one that eats *khadir*.[43] So when it (the animal) eats this until its stomach is full, it faces the sun and releases its bowels and urinates (i.e., with ease), then pastures again. And verily this money is enticing and sweet.

---

[39] Meaning that he was not an astrologer by profession, but pretended to be one in order to gain some money. The practice of astrology is itself a form of *shirk*, thus this money was tainted by the evil of astrology and the evil of cheating.

[40] *al-Mishkāt* (# 2786).

[41] *al-Mishkāt* (# 2788). It is not allowed to benefit from the animals that are given in charity unless the Muslim ruler distributes it to those that deserve it.

[42] *Sharḥ al-Arbaʿīn,* p. 275.

[43] A green crop that is not of the fanciest type of harvest.

> So how great is the Muslim companion (to it), who gives it to the poor and the orphan and the way-farer. So he who acquires it justly, and puts it in its proper place, then how great a helper it is! But he who takes it unjustly, is like the one who eats but is never satisfied, and it will be a witness against him on the Day of Judgement."[44]

In this beautiful ḥadīth, the Prophet (ﷺ) drew a parable between the one who does not care how he earns, but rather takes everything he finds, like the animal that eats from all types of crops in the spring. Spring is the season that gives crops which are generally not suitable for animals to eat. So this is an indication of a greedy person, whose only desire is to increase his or her wealth, regardless of the consequences. Such a person is never satisfied, but rather eats, and eats, and eats, until he or she is destroyed, or is almost about to be destroyed, just like the animal that eats excessively. However, the wise person chooses with care how to earn sustenance, and picks the right types of food to eat. Such a person only takes what is needed, and does not become excessively involved with earning more than the basic needs. Such a person will live a comfortable life, just like the animal that eats the right crop in moderate quantities. Furthermore, such a person will be able to earn more, when the need arises, just like this animal will be able to pasture again when it needs to. How beautiful, then, is this money when earned properly and spent properly! And how evil it is, when earned improperly, and spent improperly!

The Consequences of *Ḥarām* Sustenance

Earning through impermissible means causes great damage to a person, both in this life and in the Hereafter. Impurity does not bring about anything except impurity.

---

[44] Reported by al-Bukhārī (# 1465) and others.

The early Muslims were extremely cautious in their financial dealings. They strived their utmost to ensure that every single coin that they earned was pure and *ḥalāl*. Alas! That time has now long since disappeared. In fact, the Prophet (ﷺ) predicted,

> "A time will come in which a person will not care whether what he (earned) was through *ḥalāl* or through *ḥarām*."[45]

Unfortunately, we seem to be living in just such a time.

It is, therefore, crucial that the Muslim be aware of the evils and consequences of *ḥarām* money.

Earning through impermissible means affects a person's beliefs (*ʿaqīdah*). If person believes that it is allowed to earn sustenance through impermissible means, then this is clear disbelief, as he or she has rejected the Qur'ānic prohibitions in this regard. On the other hand, a person who trivialises this sin exposes a weakness of his *īmān* (faith). Such a person, by actions, indicates that he or she truly does not care about any reward or punishment from Allāh. The Prophet (ﷺ) has outlined the major sins, many of which deal with earning through impermissible means. Examples of such means are: eating *ribā*, taking orphan's property without just cause, taking bribes, stealing, cheating, taking possessions by force, and taking war-booty before it has been distributed properly.[46] As these limits are clear, the one who earns through impermissible means shows that he or she does not truly fear Allāh or His punishment in the Hereafter. In addition, such transgression exposes a lack of trust in Allāh, as such a person resorts to that which is *ḥarām*, not fully believing that Allāh will provide plenty through the *ḥalāl* if only the effort is exerted into achieving it through the *ḥalāl*.

Earning through impermissible means is more sinful than many of the major sins. The Prophet (ﷺ) said,

---

[45] Reported by al-Bukhārī (4/296) and others.

[46] All of these acts are reported in the authentic sunnah as being amongst the major sins. For further details, one may refer to *The Major Sins* by Imām al-Dhahabī.

> "One *dirham* (gold coin) that a person knowingly eats of *ribā* (interest) is worse than thirty-six acts of *zinā* (illegal sexual intercourse)."[47]

In another narration, he stated,

> "*Ribā* is of seventy-two types, the least of them is equivalent (i.e., in sin and filthiness) to a man having intercourse with his mother. And the greatest *ribā*, or the filthiest *ribā*, is a man defaming the honour of his Muslim brother."[48]

A Muslim who believes in the Prophet's words should ask himself, "Can earning money through interest be worth it when the Prophet (ﷺ) has compared it to having intercourse with one's mother?" In another ḥadīth, the Prophet (ﷺ) said,

> "Avoid the seven deadly sins (*al-mūbiqāt*): *shirk*, magic, killing someone without just cause, eating an orphan's property, consuming interest, accusing chaste women of fornication, and running away from the battlefield."[49]

Of these seven sins, two of them involve earning through impermissible means.

Earning through impermissible means necessitates injustice to one's family and relatives, for the father is responsible in the sight of Allāh for providing for his family. Which father, then, would come home and offer rotten and filthy meat to his wife and children? The answer, unfortunately, is many, for the filth of *ḥarām* earnings exceeds that of rotten meat. Yet, many men feel no

---

[47] Reported by Aḥmad (5/225), al-Daraquṭnī (p. 295) and others. Al-Albānī considered it authentic in his *Ghāyat al-Marām*, p. 127.

[48] Reported by al-Ṭabāranī in his *al-Awsaṭ* (1/143) and others. See *al-Silsilat al-Ṣaḥīḥah*, (# 1871). In this ḥadīth, we are also reminded of another great crime which, unfortunately, we find so common amongst our brothers and sisters, and that is to talk evil of one another, and to accuse other Muslims and defame their honour without just cause.

[49] Reported by al-Bukhārī (5/294) and Muslim (# 89).

shame in feeding such filth to their loved ones. Do they not realize that their own wives and children will be affected by this filth and impurity? And do they not realize that their own families can, on the Day of Judgement, testify against them in front of Allāh, claiming that they did not take care of them from the *ḥalāl*, but instead fed them from the *ḥarām*?

Earning through impermissible means involves injustice to others. Whether stealing, taking interest, embezzling, selling intoxicants, or whatever the transgression against the laws of Allāh may be, someone else is wronged in the process. Injustice must be done in order to earn from the *ḥarām*. The person that earns from impermissible means makes others his enemies on the Day of Judgement. In front of Allāh – the One from whom nothing is hidden – those that he has wronged will ask that justice be done. And on the Day of Judgement, the currency of trade will not be money; rather, such a person will have to give his good deeds away to those that he has wronged in order to make up for the wrong that he has done.

Earning through impermissible means puts one's good deeds at the risk of being rejected, either in totality, or in part. The Prophet (ﷺ) said,

> "O Mankind! Allāh is Pure (*al-Ṭayyib*), and He only accepts that which is pure..."[50]

Some scholars understand this ḥadīth to mean that the impure will not be accepted by Allāh, even if used for a good matter. Thus, there is a difference of opinion amongst the scholars: Will Allāh accept the prayer of a person who prays on stolen land? Or the prayer of one who prays in stolen clothes? Or the pilgrimage of one who performs Ḥajj with impure money? Some scholars state that acts such as the above will not be accepted by Allāh, and in fact, must be repeated without the impurity that contaminated them

---

[50] Reported by Muslim (# 1015) and others.

the first time. Ibn Rajab al-Ḥanbalī said, "In this ḥadīth there is a reference to the fact that no action is accepted except if one eats *ḥalāl* sustenance, and that eating *ḥarām* is a cause of having one's actions rejected."[51] (A less extreme, more widely held, and in fact more strongly supported opinion is that such acts will not necessarily be rejected, but that a person will be accountable for the sin of that which was gained through impermissible means, and rewarded for the good that was done with it. It is possible, however, that the reward gained thereby will be minimal, or even non-existent, depending on the circumstances and situation).

Earning through impermissible means is one of the surest ways that a person's *duʿā* will not be granted. Abū Hurayrah narrated that the Prophet (ﷺ) said:

> "O People! Allāh is *al-Ṭayyib* (Pure), and He only accepts that which is pure! Allāh has commanded the Believers what He has commanded the Messengers, for He said, 'O Messengers! Eat from the pure foods, and do right,' and He said, 'O you who believe! Eat from the pure and good foods We have given you.'"

Then the Prophet (ﷺ) mentioned a traveller on a long journey, who is dishevelled and dusty, and he stretches forth his hands to the sky, saying, "O my Lord! O my Lord!" – while his food is unlawful, his drink is unlawful, his clothing is unlawful, and he is nourished unlawfully; how can he (expect to) be answered?[52]

So what greater harm can their be, when a person's *duʿā* will not be responded to? The *duʿā* is the weapon of the believer. With it the believer can achieve blessings for himself and his loved ones, relief from suffering, guidance, forgiveness, and even salvation. An unjust enemy can be combated through *duʿā*, even from the other

---

[51] For further details, and this quote, see *Sharḥ al-Arbaʿīn* of Ibn Rajab al-Ḥanbalī, (1/260).

[52] Reported by Aḥmad (2/328), Muslim (2/703), and al-Tirmidhī (5/220) from Abū Hurayrah.

side of the earth. So how useless will the believer be when this weapon is taken away from him?

Earning through impermissible means causes poverty in this life. No matter how much a person earns, and how great a fortune is accumulated, if earned through *ḥarām* then Allāh will remove all blessings from such wealth. The end result is not necessarily poverty in wealth, but in life. The dissatisfied rich are all too well known, whereas the satisfied poor and middle class amongst Muslims often lead much richer and peaceful lives when all factors (such as health, happiness, contentment, productivity, family status, etc.) are taken into account. Allāh states in the Qur'ān,

وَمَآ ءَاتَيۡتُم مِّن رِّبٗا
لِّيَرۡبُوَاْ فِيٓ أَمۡوَٰلِ ٱلنَّاسِ فَلَا يَرۡبُواْ عِندَ ٱللَّهِۖ وَمَآ ءَاتَيۡتُم مِّن زَكَوٰةٖ
تُرِيدُونَ وَجۡهَ ٱللَّهِ فَأُوْلَٰٓئِكَ هُمُ ٱلۡمُضۡعِفُونَ ٣٩

> "And that which you give as interest, so that you may increase (your wealth) from the property of other people, has no increase with Allāh. But that which you give in *zakāt*, seeking the Pleasure of Allāh, then those shall have a manifold increase." [Sūrah *al-Rūm*, 39]

Likewise, the Prophet (ﷺ) said,

> "No one increases his dealings in *ribā* (interest) except that the end of his affairs will be paucity."[53]

Earning through impermissible means brings about the curse of Allāh and His Messenger, and what a dark and dismal future such a curse would portend. For what hope can one expect for the person whom the Lord of the creation and His most beloved Messenger have cursed? The Prophet (ﷺ) cursed the one who

---

[53] Reported by Ibn Mājah (# 2279). Al-Būṣayrī said that its chain is authentic, and Ibn Ḥajr said the same, as did al-Albānī in *Ṣaḥīḥ al-Jāmi'* (# 5518).

eats *ribā*, the one who gives it, the one who writes (the contract), and the two witnesses. In this regard, he said,

"They are all equivalent (in sin)."[54]

So all the parties involved in a contract containing *ribā* are equivalent in sin, and all of them are cursed upon the tongue of the Prophet (ﷺ). Furthermore, he (ﷺ) also stated,

> "Allāh has cursed intoxicants, and the one that drinks it, and the one that pours it, and the one that sells it, and the one that buys it, and the one that produces it, and the one for whom it is produced, and the one that carries it, and the one to whom it is carried,"

and in another narration,

> "The Prophet (ﷺ) cursed ten people with regards to intoxicants: the one that produces it, and the one for whom it is produced, and the one that drinks it, and the one that carries it, and the one to whom it is carried, and the one that pours it, and the one that sells it, and the one who eats its price, and the one who buys it, and the one for whom it is bought."[55]

Out of ten categories of sin regarding alcohol, four of them are directly related to the transaction and trade of intoxicants.

Earning through impermissible means incurs the displeasure of Allāh, and prohibits things that are allowed. As the transgressor forsakes the lawful voluntarily, so too might Allāh send down punishment in the form of further restrictions upon the lawful. In essence, Allāh may choose to punish transgressors by the exact same pathway of their own choosing. Those who transgress into intoxicants may be given more, to the point that their lives are ruined on alcohol and drugs. Those who transgress into the

---

[54] Reported by Muslim (# 1598) and others.

[55] Reported by al-Tirmidhī (# 1295), Ibn Mājah (# 3383) and others. Al-Albānī declared it to be authentic in *al-Mishkāt*, (# 2776 and 2777).

sexually forbidden may find seductions made easy for them, right up to the day they break out with the manifestation of AIDS. Similarly, those who earn the unlawful may find unlawful earnings made easy for them, and the lawful progressively more difficult to achieve. Lessons can be learnt from the nations before us. The Children of Israel used to be a favoured nation, and Allāh bestowed blessings upon them which He bestowed on no other nation. Yet, despite this preferred status, Allāh's curse fell upon them when they started earning from impermissible methods. Subsequently, many pure things were prohibited upon them as a punishment for their sins. Allāh says,

فَبِظُلْمٍ مِّنَ ٱلَّذِينَ هَادُوا۟
حَرَّمْنَا عَلَيْهِمْ طَيِّبَٰتٍ أُحِلَّتْ لَهُمْ وَبِصَدِّهِمْ عَن سَبِيلِ ٱللَّهِ
كَثِيرًا ﴿١٦٠﴾ وَأَخْذِهِمُ ٱلرِّبَوٰا۟ وَقَدْ نُهُوا۟ عَنْهُ وَأَكْلِهِمْ أَمْوَٰلَ ٱلنَّاسِ
بِٱلْبَٰطِلِ ۚ وَأَعْتَدْنَا لِلْكَٰفِرِينَ مِنْهُمْ عَذَابًا أَلِيمًا ﴿١٦١﴾

> "For the wrong-doing of the Jews, We made unlawful to them certain good foods which had been lawful to them, and for their hindering many from Allāh's Way. And their taking of interest (*ribā*), even though they were forbidden from taking it, and their devouring people's wealth wrongfully. And We have prepared for the disbelievers among them a painful torment." [Sūrah *al-Nisā*, 160 – 161]

And in an authentic narration, the Prophet (ﷺ) said,

> "Allāh's curse is on the Jews. When Allāh prohibited upon them the fat of the animals, they dissolved it,[56] then sold it and ate its price!"[57]

Earning through impermissible means is equivalent to eating fire. Allāh states,

---

[56] Meaning they transformed it into something that could be utilised, such as grease or oil.

[57] Reported by al-Bukhārī (# 2236), Muslim (3/1207) and others.

إِنَّ ٱلَّذِينَ يَأْكُلُونَ أَمْوَٰلَ ٱلْيَتَٰمَىٰ ظُلْمًا إِنَّمَا يَأْكُلُونَ فِى
بُطُونِهِمْ نَارًا ۖ وَسَيَصْلَوْنَ سَعِيرًا ﴿١٠﴾

"Verily, those who unjustly eat up the property of orphans, they eat up only a fire into their bellies, and they will be burnt in the blazing Fire!" [Sūrah *al-Nisā*, 10]

So he who provides his family with *ḥarām* should ask himself: does he want to provide himself and his family the fire of Hell?

Earning through impermissible means can bring severe punishments on the Day of Judgement and in the Hereafter. Ponder over the severe punishment that awaits he who sells his merchandise dishonestly, with false oaths. The Prophet (ﷺ) said,

"Three people, Allāh will not (even) look at them on the Day of Judgement, nor will He purify them, and they will have a severe punishment!"

He repeated this three times. Abū Dharr said, "They are destroyed and lost, O Messenger of Allāh! Who are they?" He replied,

"The *musbil*,[58] the *mannān*,[59] and the one who sells his merchandise with a false oath."[60]

In another narration of Abū Hurayrah, the Prophet (ﷺ) said,

"Three (people), Allāh will not speak to them on the Day of Judgement, nor will He look at them, nor will he purify them, and they will have a severe punishment: a person who had extra water in a strange land (i.e., while travelling), and he did not give it to (other) travellers; and a person who sold an

---

[58] A *musbil* is one who lowers his garments below his ankles. This act is prohibited for men only.

[59] The *mannān* is one who always reminds others of the favours and good that he has done for them.

[60] Reported by Muslim (# 289) and others.

> item to another person after *ʿAṣr*,[61] swearing to him by Allāh that he had purchased it for such and such (a price), while that was not the case; and a person who swore allegiance to a ruler only for the sake of this world, if he was given of it, he will fulfil his oath, and if he were prevented from it, then he will break it."[62]

So those who sell their merchandise with false promises will await a severe punishment on the Day of Judgement. Allāh will not even look at them (for the one whom Allāh looks at receives His Mercy, whereas the one whom Allāh turns away from is condemned), nor will He speak to them a speech of mercy, nor will He purify them of their sins, and they will face a severe punishment in the Fire of Hell. The same can be said for those who knowingly advertise their product in such a way as to makes it appear better than it truly is.

Earning through impermissible means is a cause of humiliation for the entire Muslim nation. This is because it destroys the fabric of honesty that clothes a true Muslim society with integrity. The Prophet (ﷺ) said,

> "If you deal in *ʿīyna*,[63] and hold fast to the tails of cows, and become content with agriculture, and leave *jihād*, then Allāh

---

[61] The reason that this specific time is mentioned is because it is a blessed time, for the angels come down and ascend after the *ʿAṣr* prayer. This of course does not imply that it is allowed to swear falsely at other times! See *al-Minhāj Sharḥ Ṣaḥīḥ Muslim* (1/300).

[62] Reported by Muslim (# 293) and others.

[63] *ʿĪyna* is a transaction that appears to be permissible, but in reality is a trick to get around interest; it is therefore prohibited. It occurs when a person sells an item to another person for a deferred price, and then buys it back from him for a lower, immediate price. So, in reality, he has given him some money, and expects back a higher amount later on. The actual item that was sold returns to the original owner, and was used to try to 'get out' of interest.

will inflict upon you a humiliation that will never be removed from you until you return to your religion."[64]

So when the use of *'īyna* becomes rampant in society, then Allāh will take away the honour and prestige that the Muslims are entitled to enjoy. And if this is the case with *'īyna* – which is one of the slightest and most hidden forms of *ribā* – then what will be the case when Muslims are openly dealing with interest and increasing their wealth – without the least shame – through impermissible ways? Do we not, as Muslims, realize the reason that we are undergoing such world-wide humiliations and afflictions is because we have transgressed the boundaries of our religion? Because we are earning by *ribā*, content with earning money by any means, and abandoning the struggle to establish Allāh's religion, not just in the land, but even in our own meagre selves?

Earning through impermissible means makes it *ḥarām* for a person to enter Paradise, and is a cause for being cast into the fire of Hell. The Prophet (ﷺ) said to one of the Companions,

> "O Ka'ab ibn 'Ujrah! Any flesh that has been fed on *suḥt* will never enter Paradise! And any flesh that has been fed on *suḥt* has more right to go to the fire of Hell."

In another phrase,

> "Any flesh that has been nourished with *ḥarām* will not enter Paradise,"

and in another narration,

[64] Reported by Abū Dāwūd (# 3462) and others, and declared acceptable (*jayyid*) by Ibn Taymiyyah (*Majmū' al-Fatāwa,* 29/20); Aḥmad Shākir and al-Albānī declared it *Ṣaḥīḥ* (*Silsilah al-Ṣaḥīḥah*, # 11).

"Any flesh that has grown on *suḥt...*"[65]

The word '*suḥt*' has been defined by al-Rāghib al-Isfahanī as, '...every prohibited object which causes disgrace to the one that does it, as if it removes (*yusḥitu*) his religion and good character.'[66] Therefore, these ḥadīths imply that any and all types of impure wealth are a cause of entering the fire of Hell, and prohibit one from entering Paradise.[67]

The above list is long, but represents only a partial inventory of the dangers of *ḥarām* earning. The weight and implications

---

[65] This ḥadīth has been reported from the *musnad* of Ibn ʿAbbās, Jābir ibn ʿAbdillāh, Ka'ab ibn ʿUjrah, and Abū Bakr. The ḥadīth of Ibn ʿAbbās is reported in al-Ṭabāranī in his *Muʿjam al-Kabīr* (11/174), but in its chain is a rejected narrator. The ḥadīth of Jābir ibn ʿAbdillāh is the strongest, and is reported by ʿAbd al-Razzāq in his *al-Muṣannaf* (11/345), and through him al-Ḥākim in his *al-Mustadrak* (4/422). Al-Ḥākim declared it *Ṣaḥīḥ* and al-Dhahabī agreed with him, but it appears that it is *ḥasan* due to one the narrators. The ḥadīth of Ka'ab ibn ʿUjrah has been reported by many weak chains, but together they are acceptable as supporting evidence, and perhaps reach the level of *ḥasan* (Ibn ʿAbd al-Barr in his *al-Tamhīd* [5/401] reported it from Ibn ʿAbbās; al-Ṭabāranī in his *Muʿjam al-Kabīr* reported it from Ṭāriq ibn Shihab [9/106], ʿĀsim al-ʿAdwī [9/136] and Abū Bakr ibn Bashīr [19/162] – all four of them from Ka'ab). The narration of Abū Bakr is recorded by al-Bayhaqī in *Shuʿab al-Īmān* and Abū Nuʿaym in his *Ḥilya*, and al-Manāwī said, 'Its chain is weak.' Al-Tabrīzī recorded two of these narrations in his *al-Mishkāt* (# 2772 and 2787), but al-Albānī did not give any comments on it in his checking of the *Mishkāt*; however, he did mention it in his *Ṣaḥīḥ al-Jāmi'* (# 4519). It appears that the ḥadīth is at least *ḥasan li-ghayrihi* due to all of its various chains, and Allāh knows best.

[66] *Al-Mufradāt*, p. 400.

[67] This of course does not mean eternal damnation to the Fire, as nothing except *kufr* and its equivalents subject a person to eternal banishment from Paradise. These ḥadīth are understood in light of all other pertinent texts, and the meaning is that a person who eats from *ḥarām* will not enter Paradise until he or she passes a period of time in the Fire of Hell, unless Allāh chooses otherwise and grants forgiveness.

of these evidences are overpowering. People of true and sincere belief must recognise that *ḥarām* money can never purchase lasting pleasure, for the severity and duration of the punishment of the transgressors in both this life and the next far outweigh any transient pleasures of this world.

So ponder over these texts from the Qur'ān and sunnah, and ask yourself, O Muslim, 'Is it worthwhile for me to get involved with interest, and stealing, and selling prohibited materials such as intoxicants and pornography, and all other *ḥarām* methods of gaining money? Will this money truly bring me happiness in this life, or in the Hereafter? Or will it only be a cause of my griefs and sorrows, and eventually lead to my destruction?'

The True Richness

Many people mistakenly assume that true wealth and real treasure is that of money. It is indeed true that wealth is a great blessing from Allāh which He bestows upon His servants. And the one who earns it purely, and spends it properly, and gives it to those that deserve it, without a doubt earns a great reward from Allāh.

But at the same time, wealth is not the greatest blessing that can be given to mankind. Furthermore, no matter how much wealth a person has, eventually it will leave him, and pass on into the hands of others. The Prophet (ﷺ) reminded us of this when he asked the Companions,

> "Who amongst you loves the money of his inheritors more than his own money?"[68]

---

[68] In other words, who amongst you loves the money that is in the hands of the people who will inherit from him when he dies (such as one's sons and daughters) more than the money that he himself owns.

They replied, "O Messenger of Allāh! There is no one of us except that he loves his own money more than he loves the money of his inheritors." So the Prophet (ﷺ) replied,

> "But his money is only that which he sent forth, and the money of his inheritors is what he left behind."[69]

So in reality most of the money that a person owns will eventually end up in the hands of his or her inheritors, and only that part which was spent for the sake of Allāh will actually benefit one in the hereafter.

Allāh emphasizes this point in the Qur'ān with the teaching that,

ٱلْمَالُ وَٱلْبَنُونَ زِينَةُ ٱلْحَيَوٰةِ ٱلدُّنْيَا ۖ وَٱلْبَٰقِيَٰتُ ٱلصَّٰلِحَٰتُ
خَيْرٌ عِندَ رَبِّكَ ثَوَابًا وَخَيْرٌ أَمَلًا ﴿٤٦﴾

> "Wealth and children are the adornments of the life of this world. But the permanent righteous deeds are better in your Lord's Sight (to attain) rewards, and better in respect of hope." [Sūrah *al-Kahf*, 46]

So money and children can be a comfort and a pleasure of this life, but righteous deeds are what will remain permanently – not one's family or wealth. It is these righteous deeds which will bring a person Allāh's Pleasure, and through which a person can hope for an ever-lasting reward in the Hereafter. The Qur'ān clearly states,

وَمَآ أَمْوَٰلُكُمْ وَلَآ أَوْلَٰدُكُم بِٱلَّتِى تُقَرِّبُكُمْ عِندَنَا
زُلْفَىٰٓ إِلَّا مَنْ ءَامَنَ وَعَمِلَ صَٰلِحًا فَأُو۟لَٰٓئِكَ لَهُمْ جَزَآءُ ٱلضِّعْفِ
بِمَا عَمِلُوا۟ وَهُمْ فِى ٱلْغُرُفَٰتِ ءَامِنُونَ ﴿٣٧﴾

---

[69] Reported by al-Bukhārī (4/217) and others.

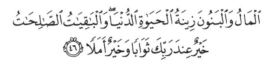

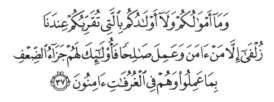

"And it is not your wealth, nor your children that bring you nearer to Us, but only he (will please Us) who believes, and does righteous deeds; for such (people), there will be a double reward for what they did, and they will reside in the high dwellings (of Paradise), in peace and security." [Sūrah *Saba'*, 37]

The great student of Ibn 'Abbās, Qatādah al-Sadūsi, said commenting on this verse, "So do not judge people based on the amount of money and children they have! Even a disbeliever might be given money, whereas the Muslim has been withheld from it."[70]

In a well-known and oft-repeated parable, the Qur'ān compares the life of this world to a crop that flourishes after rainfall, only to wither up and shrivel in a short period of time. The Qur'ān states,

اعْلَمُوا أَنَّمَا الْحَيَوٰةُ
الدُّنْيَا لَعِبٌ وَلَهْوٌ وَزِينَةٌ وَتَفَاخُرٌ بَيْنَكُمْ وَتَكَاثُرٌ فِي الْأَمْوَٰلِ
وَالْأَوْلَٰدِ كَمَثَلِ غَيْثٍ أَعْجَبَ الْكُفَّارَ نَبَاتُهُ ثُمَّ يَهِيجُ فَتَرَىٰهُ
مُصْفَرًّا ثُمَّ يَكُونُ حُطَٰمًا وَفِي الْآخِرَةِ عَذَابٌ شَدِيدٌ وَمَغْفِرَةٌ
مِّنَ اللَّهِ وَرِضْوَٰنٌ وَمَا الْحَيَوٰةُ الدُّنْيَا إِلَّا مَتَٰعُ الْغُرُورِ ﴿٢٠﴾

"Realize that the life of this world is only play and amusement, pomp and mutual boasting among you, and rivalry in respect of wealth and children. It is like the vegetation (that sprouts forth) after rain, whose growth is pleasing to the disbeliever. Soon it dries up, and you see it turning yellow, then it becomes straw. But in the Hereafter (there is) a severe torment (for the disbelievers), and (there is) Forgiveness from Allāh and (His) Good Pleasure (for the believers). And indeed, the life of this world is only a deceiving enjoyment." [Sūrah *Ḥadīd,* 20]

---

[70] Reported by al-Ṭabarī in his *Tafsīr*.

Imām al-Saʿadī summarised the commentary of this verse when he wrote, in a very beautiful passage:

> In this verse, Allāh informs us of the true nature of this world, and what it is really based on, and He explains its end, and the end of the people in it. He informs us that it is a mere play and amusement, so our bodies play in it, and our hearts are amused at it. And we see that this is exactly what the people that are following this world are upon, so you find that they have wasted their entire lives so that they can amuse their hearts. They are in total ignorance about remembering Allāh, and what they are about to face of rewards and punishments (in the Hereafter). You see them taking their religion as an amusement and pastime.
>
> And this is in contrast to the people of awareness, and the ones that strive for the Hereafter. Their hearts are alive with the remembrance of Allāh, and His knowledge, and His love. And they have busied themselves with actions that will bring them closer to Allāh, whether those actions will benefit themselves only, or also others. And the phrase, '...*zīnah*...,' or 'pompness,' means that they will try to beautify themselves in their clothes, food, drinks, the means of transportation, their houses and palaces, their prestige, and other matters. The phrase, '...mutual boasting amongst you...,' implies that everyone is attached (to this world), trying to outdo others, so that he will be the victor in all its matters. He wishes that he can satisfy all of his desires through it. And (this occurs in money and children), so each one wants to be the one that has more than the other, in money and children. And this is what is occurring amongst those that love this world and are content with it.
>
> But this is in contrast to the one who realizes this world and its reality, so he made it a passage, and not the goal. So he competed in coming closer to Allāh, and he took the necessary means to ensure that he would arrive at the promised destination. So when he sees someone who tries to compete with him in money and children, he instead competes against him with good deeds!

Then, Allāh drew for us a parable of this world. It is like a rain that falls to the earth, and then mixes with the vegetation that is eaten by men and animals, until, when the earth spreads forth is beauty, and the disbelievers – those who cannot see beyond this life – are amazed at its fruits, the command of Allāh comes upon it. So it is destroyed, and it withers up, and dries, and it returns to its previous state, as if the land never gave any greenery, and as if no beauty were ever seen on it!

And this is how this world is! While it is at its prime for its companion, sprouting forth with beauty, whatever he wants of its treasures he can take, and whenever he wants to obtain anything of it, he finds the doors to achieve it are open, when, all of a sudden, Allāh's decree falls upon it. So all of it is removed from his hands, and his control over it is gone, or he himself is removed from it, so he leaves it with absolutely nothing of it in his hands, having gained nothing from all of it except a shroud (that is placed on the dead body). So woe to him who makes it his goal, and sacrifices everything for it, and strives and devotes his entire life to it!

And as for the actions of the Hereafter, then that is what will truly benefit. It will store for its owner (the fruits of his work), and will accompany him forever. This is why Allāh stated, 'But in the Hereafter (there is) a severe torment (for the disbelievers), and (there is) Forgiveness from Allāh and (His) Good Pleasure (for the believers).' So, the Hereafter will be one of these two matters only.

As for the punishment, then it will be in the Fire of Hell, and its pits and chains, and all of its horrors. And this will be for one who has made this world his goal, and the end of his journey, so he freely disobeyed Allāh, and rejected His signs, and did not thank His blessings.

And as for the forgiveness from Allāh for one's sins, and the absolvement of all punishment, and the pleasure of Allāh, then this will be for one who strived for the Abode of Enjoyment (Paradise) – the one who realised the true nature of this world, and therefore strived a real striving for the Hereafter.

So all of this should make us lessen our desire for this world, and increase our desire for the Hereafter, and this is why Allāh said, 'And indeed, the life of this world is only a deceiving enjoyment.' So, this (life) is an enjoyment that a person can benefit from, and take his needs from. No one except a person of weak mind will be deceived by it, and become content with it, and these are the ones that Allāh will allow to be deceived by the Deceiver (*Shayṭān*).[71]

No matter how much money a person earns, in reality he only utilizes a very small fraction of it. Ponder over the wise reminder from the Prophet (ﷺ). ʿAbdullāh ibn al-Shakhīr reported, "I entered upon the Prophet (ﷺ) and he was reciting "*Alhākum al-takāthur*"(The mutual rivalry [for trying to compete with one another in worldly matters] diverts you) [al-Takāthur; 1]. He said,

> 'The son of Ādam cries out: "My money! My money!" But do you have, O son of Ādam, anything of your money, except that which you eat, so it is wasted, or that which you wear, so it wears out, or that which you gave as charity, so you have sent it forth (to get its rewards in the Hereafter)?'"[72]

In this ḥadīth, the Prophet (ﷺ) reminded us that, in reality, all of our money is utilised in only three ways. Firstly, the food that we eat, and this eventually is transformed into waste product. Secondly, the clothes that we wear, and this eventually wears out so that it is unusable. Thirdly, the money that has been spent for the sake of Allāh, and this is the only part whose benefits remain and return to us. So of what benefit is it for a person to gloat over 'his money', and boast about it, and be eager for it, when in reality so little of it is actually spent in such a way as to provide eternal benefit?

---

[71] *Tafsīr al-Saʿadī*, pps. 780-781.

[72] Reported by Muslim (8/211) and others.

Because of these factors, the Prophet Muḥammad (ﷺ) reminded mankind that wealth is not proportionate to the amount of material possessions a person owns. True wealth is to be content with what one has, and then to use it to strive for the everlasting reward of the Hereafter. The Prophet (ﷺ) said,

> "Richness is not in the quantity of possessions (that one has); rather, true richness is the richness of one's self (or contentment)."[73]

He (ﷺ) also stated,

> "That which is little yet sufficient is better than that which is much but distracts."[74]

And in a third ḥadīth,

> "He is indeed successful who has been guided to Islām, and his sustenance was sufficient for him, and he was content with it."[75]

Lastly,

> "The best sustenance that you are given is that which is sufficient."[76]

So true success and wealth is found in the peace and satisfaction which results from sincerity in faith and practice. The contentment of the heart is what makes a person realise and appreciate this true richness. The Prophet (ﷺ) described this richness in another ḥadīth, where he said,

> "Whoever amongst you wakes up, secure in his house, healthy in his body, having the bare amount of food that he requires

---

[73] Reported by al-Bukhārī (4/219) and others.

[74] Reported by Abū Ya'lā (1/295), Ibn Adī (7/2)and others, and al-Albānī authenticated it in *al-Ṣaḥīḥah*, (# 947).

[75] Reported by Muslim (3/102) and others.

[76] Reported by Ibn Ḥibbān (# 2323). See *al-Silsilah al-Ṣaḥīḥah*, (# 1834).

for the day, then it is as if the entire world has been captured for him, with all that it contains!"[77]

This ḥadīth has many benefits that can be obtained from it. '*Whoever amongst you...*,' means the Muslims, indicating the first and greatest blessing, namely, that of Islām; '*...wakes up...*,' means that one has been blessed with life; '*...secure in his house...*,' means without fear of attack upon one's safety or the safety of one's family; '*...healthy in his body...*,' means that Allāh has saved him or her from diseases and sicknesses; '*...having the bare amount of food that he requires for the day...*' indicates that even the minimal amount of sustenance is a great blessing from Allāh, for this is what the body and health requires, and many people do not even have this amount; and lastly, '*...it is as if the entire world has been captured for him, with all that it contains*,' indicating that this is all that a person needs of this life, and everything that is in addition to this bare minimum is an unnecessary luxury.

Contentment with Allāh's provision, whether large or small, is contentment with life, and hence, the best wealth that a person can have. The Prophet (ﷺ) stated,

> "Verily Allāh tests His servant with what He has given him. So whoever is content with whatever he has been assigned, then Allāh will bless him in it, and give him more! But whoever is not content (with what he has been given), then he will not be blessed in it."[78]

Those who are content with their own provision and lot in life will lose concern over the wealth and status of others. Such people have no concern as to how much money others have, what types of

---

[77] Reported by al-Tirmidhī (# 2347) who considered it *ḥasan gharīb*; al-Bukhārī in his *al-Adab al-Mufrad* (# 300), Ibn Ḥibbān in his *Taqasīm* (# 2507) and others. Al-Albānī agreed with al-Tirmidhī in his *Silsilah* (# 2318).

[78] Reported by Aḥmad (5/24), with an authentic chain, as mentioned in *al-Ṣaḥīḥah*, (# 1658).

cars they drives, or the size of the houses they live in. Those with clean hearts in this respect love Allāh, and are grateful to Him, knowing that the goods of this world cannot buy happiness, or the blessings of faith and contentment. In return, they are loved by Allāh, and by fellow men and women. This principle is so clearly outlined in the noble Prophetic tradition:

> "Give up (hope of attaining) this world, Allāh will love you. And give up (hope of) whatever is in the possession of other people, and the people will love you."[79]

In another narration, a person came to the Prophet (ﷺ) and asked him, "O Messenger of Allāh! Narrate to me a ḥadīth, and make it short!" So he (ﷺ) replied,

> "Pray your prayer as if it is your last, as if you are seeing Him (Allāh), for even if you do not see Him then He sees you. And give up hope (of obtaining) what other's possess, then you will live a rich life. And beware of anything that you might (later) have to make an excuse for."[80]

So whoever sets as a primary goal the pleasure of Allāh and the rewards of the Hereafter will be loved by Allāh, and whoever avoids competing with fellow Muslims concerning worldly matters will be loved by the people. And this wealth – the love of Allāh and that of mankind – is far greater than any richness that money can buy.

---

[79] Reported by Ibn Mājah (# 4102), al-Ḥākim (4/313) who considered it *Ṣaḥīḥ*, and others. Al-Albānī also graded it as authentic in *al-Silsilah*, (# 944).

[80] Reported by al-Bukhārī in his *al-Tārīkh* (3/216), and al-Ṭabārānī in his *al-Awsaṭ* (# 4588) and others. Al-Haythamī, in his *Majmaʿ al-Zawāʾid* (10/229) said: "There are, in its chain, people that I do not know." However, this narration has supporting evidences, including the ḥadīth of Saʿd ibn Abī Waqqās, and ʿAbdullāh ibn Masʿūd (in al-Ṭabārānī's *al-Awsaṭ*, # 5907), due to which al-Albānī considered it acceptable in his *al-Ṣaḥīḥah* (# 1914).

The pious predecessors of this nation also realised this principle. Awn ibn 'Abdillāh[81] said, "The greatest blessing is that – when this world is straightened for you – you appreciate what you have been given of the blessings of Islām."[82] So next time you are in severe financial circumstances, instead of looking at the material and temporary pleasures that you have not been afforded, ponder instead over the treasure of *īmān* that Allāh has blessed you with, and appreciate the great fortune of being a Muslim!

Likewise, when you are overjoyed or distressed due to some monetary gain or loss, remember the statement of Muḥammad ibn Sūqah[83], who said, "There are two characteristics which, even though Allāh does not punish us for them, are reason enough for our punishment: we are overjoyed at a small gain that we receive from this world, and yet Allāh has never seen us so happy for a good deed that we do, and we are so worried about a small matter that has missed us concerning this world, and yet Allāh has never seen us so worried about a sin that we commit."[84]

This section is concluded by quoting the verse in which Allāh reminded the Prophet (ﷺ) and the believers not to long for the wealth of this world – wealth that has been given to those that have rejected submission to Allāh – but rather to strive for the richness of the Hereafter:

---

[81] The grand-nephew of 'Abdullāh ibn Mas'ūd. When he used to narrate ḥadīth, his beard would become wet with tears. He died around 115 A.H. (see *Tahdhīb al-Tahdhīb*, 3/338).

[82] Ibn Abī al-Dunyā, *al-Qanā'ah wa al-Ta'afuf*, (# 151).

[83] Of the major students of the *tabi'īn*. Sufyān ibn'Uyaynah said, "There were three people in *Kūfah*, if they were told, 'You are going to die tomorrow' they would not have been able to increase any of their good deeds (due to the fact that they were doing so many). Of them is Muḥammad ibn Sūqah." (See *Tahdhīb al-Tahdhīb*, 3/584).

[84] Ibn Abī al-Dunyā, *al-Qanā'ah wa al-Ta'afuf*, (# 153).

وَلَا تَمُدَّنَّ عَيْنَيْكَ إِلَىٰ مَا مَتَّعْنَا بِهِۦٓ أَزْوَٰجًا مِّنْهُمْ زَهْرَةَ ٱلْحَيَوٰةِ ٱلدُّنْيَا لِنَفْتِنَهُمْ فِيهِ ۚ وَرِزْقُ رَبِّكَ خَيْرٌ وَأَبْقَىٰ ﴿١٣١﴾

> "And strain not your eyes in longing for the things that We have given for enjoyment to various groups of them (the disbelievers) - the splendour of the life of this world - that We may test them thereby. And indeed, the provision (*rizq*) of your Lord is better and more lasting." [Sūrah *Ṭā Hā*, 131]

The Wisdom of Disparity

As soon as children are able to comprehend their surroundings, they are made aware of the fact that not all of mankind is at the same level and status. They see those who are so poor that they do not even have a roof over their heads, and they also see those who live in mighty palaces and mansions.

إِنَّ رَبَّكَ يَبْسُطُ ٱلرِّزْقَ لِمَن يَشَآءُ وَيَقْدِرُ ۚ إِنَّهُۥ كَانَ بِعِبَادِهِۦ خَبِيرًۢا بَصِيرًا ﴿٣٠﴾

> "Truly, your Lord enlarges the provision for whom He wills, and straitens (for whom He wills). Verily, He is the All-Knower, All-Seer of His slaves." [Sūrah *al-Isrā*, 30]

It is Allāh who decides and decrees how much to give each soul. It is He who is the All-Seer and All-Knower, for He knows who deserves to be blessed with how much in this life and in the Hereafter. So all of Allāh's decrees are praiseworthy. If He gives to some, it is out of His Infinite Wisdom, and if He withholds from others, then that too is out of His Infinite Wisdom.

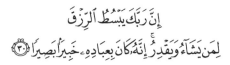

أَهُمْ
يَقْسِمُونَ رَحْمَتَ رَبِّكَ ۚ نَحْنُ قَسَمْنَا بَيْنَهُم مَّعِيشَتَهُمْ فِي الْحَيَاةِ
الدُّنْيَا ۚ وَرَفَعْنَا بَعْضَهُمْ فَوْقَ بَعْضٍ دَرَجَاتٍ لِّيَتَّخِذَ بَعْضُهُم
بَعْضًا سُخْرِيًّا ۗ وَرَحْمَتُ رَبِّكَ خَيْرٌ مِّمَّا يَجْمَعُونَ ﴿٣٢﴾

"Is it they who would portion out the Mercy of your Lord? It is We Who portion out between them their livelihood in this world, and We raised some of them above others in ranks, so that some may employ others in their work. But the Mercy of your Lord (O Muḥammad) is better than the (wealth of this world) which they amass." [Sūrah *al-Zukhruf*, 32]

In another verse, Allāh reminds us:

وَاللَّهُ
فَضَّلَ بَعْضَكُمْ عَلَىٰ بَعْضٍ فِي الرِّزْقِ ۚ فَمَا الَّذِينَ فُضِّلُوا بِرَادِّي
رِزْقِهِمْ عَلَىٰ مَا مَلَكَتْ أَيْمَانُهُمْ فَهُمْ فِيهِ سَوَاءٌ ۚ أَفَبِنِعْمَةِ
اللَّهِ يَجْحَدُونَ ﴿٧١﴾

"And Allāh has preferred some of you above others in wealth and properties. Then, those who are preferred will by no means hand over their wealth (and properties) to those (slaves) whom their right hands possess, so that they may be equal with them in (that) respect. Do they then deny the Favour of Allāh."[Sūrah *al-Naḥl*, 71]

It is possible that a person, were he to be given more wealth, would use it to rebel against the commandants of Allāh. Therefore, the very confinement of wealth might be one of the greatest blessings given to a particular person.

وَلَوْ بَسَطَ اللَّهُ الرِّزْقَ
لِعِبَادِهِ لَبَغَوْا فِي الْأَرْضِ وَلَٰكِن يُنَزِّلُ بِقَدَرٍ مَّا يَشَاءُ ۚ إِنَّهُ بِعِبَادِهِ
خَبِيرٌ بَصِيرٌ ﴿٢٧﴾

> "And if Allāh were to enlarge the provision for His slaves, they would surely rebel in the earth, but He sends down by measure as He wills. Verily! He is in respect of His slaves, the Well-Aware, the All-Seer (of things that benefit them)." [Sūrah *al-Shūra*, 27]

Once, Sa'ad ibn Abī Waqqās was sitting with the Prophet (ﷺ) while money was being distributed to the poor. The Prophet (ﷺ) gave money to certain people, and withheld from others. At this, Sa'ad said, "O Messenger of Allāh! Why do you not give to so-and-so, for, by Allāh, I see him to be a believer." At this, the Prophet (ﷺ) remained silent, until Sa'ad repeated his request three times. The Prophet (ﷺ) then replied,

> "O Sa'ad! I give to a certain person, even though others are more beloved to me than him, for fear that Allāh might throw him into the Fire of Hell."[85]

In other words, the Prophet (ﷺ) felt that by giving money to certain people, they would be tempted to use it in ways that were not permissible. Thus, it was for their benefit not to be given such money.

The Qur'ān refers to some of the wisdoms behind the differences in wealth and status. In addition, there are benefits that can be inferred when one contemplates the nature of human society. Some of these benefits are as follows:

1) The clear proof that Allāh is the One who is in charge of the affairs of His creation. He is the *Rabb*, the Creator, Nourisher and Sustainer. How else is it that every single living object is provided for and taken care of?

2) The proof that Allāh is the Ever-Wise, for He decides and decrees the exact amount of sustenance for His servants.

3) An indication of the complete Power of Allāh over His

[85] Reported by al-Bukhārī (# 27), Muslim (# 150), and others.

creation, for no one can alter His Decree. So you find a person, struggling his or her entire life to become rich, only to die as a pauper. And here is another one who, without any effort, is blessed with wealth that others only dream of. All of this is an indication that Allāh is capable of all things.

4) The great mercy that is shown to all of mankind through these different levels of wealth. Had it not been for the fact that mankind is of different levels, then no one would have served another, nor would any affair or matter be taken care of by another. It is only because of the fact that certain people have more wealth than others that they will use their wealth to gain certain efforts from others. Had it not been for this disparity, no one would take up any profession, and the entire society would be harmed.

5) This disparity brings out the kindness of the pious Muslim, and the miserliness of everyone else. For the true Muslim will use this money and be generous to the poor. Such a Muslim will spend hard-earned money on his family, relatives, and acquaintances, not expecting any reward from them, but rather from Allāh.

6) The great test and trial that every single person must display if he wishes to gain the pleasure of Allāh. So the poor beggar must be patient in his adversity, and accept the decree of Allāh, while the rich one must also be patient, and not follow his every whim and desire with the money that he has been given. Money and other forms of wealth is one of the greatest ways in which mankind is tested, so that they can be rewarded or punished according to their deeds.

7) Every person has a particular 'limit' on his or her level of restraint. It is possible that a particular person, if blessed with a large amount of wealth, would not be able to control illicit urgings, and thus disobey Allāh with such wealth. Therefore, the fact that Allāh has *not* blessed such people with so much wealth is a manifestation of Allāh's Mercy towards them.

8) Had everyone been blessed with wealth, they would have transgressed and become arrogant, spreading evil in the land. By differentiating between people, Allāh has ensured that such transgression, even if it occurs, is not permanent or universal.

So the pious Muslim accepts what Allāh has pre-destined, and follows the advice of the Prophet (ﷺ) when said,

> "Look at those who are below you (in status and wealth), and do not look at those who are above you, because then it is more likely that you will not trivialise the blessings of Allāh upon you."[86]

[86] Reported by al-Bukhārī (# 2275) and others.

The Ways of Increasing Wealth

The Qur'ān and sunnah have informed us of certain acts that cause an increase in one's wealth. Below are fifteen such acts which are guaranteed to cause financial increase in this world – if done properly and for the sake of Allāh.[87]

i. The *Taqwa* of Allāh

One of the primary ways to increase one's *rizq* is to increase one's *taqwa* of Allāh. Therefore, we first must define and understand *taqwa* before discussing the proofs for this claim.

The Meaning of Taqwa

Imām al-Rāghib al-Isfahānī defined *taqwa* as, "...guarding one's self from sins, and this is achieved by leaving all blameworthy acts, and it is perfected by leaving some permissible acts."[88] Al-Ḥāfiẓ al-Nawawī stated that it is to, "...implement (the Divine) commands and prohibitions. And its essence is to protect yourself from His punishment and anger, all Glory be to Him."[89] The famous student of Ibn 'Abbās, Mujāhid ibn Jabr defined *taqwa* as, "It is that you obey Allāh, so that He is never disobeyed, and

[87] Much of this section has been translated from Dr. Faḍl Elahi's work *Mafātīḥ al-Rizq*. Dr. Elahi mentions ten ways in his tract, and from other sources I found five other ways.

[88] *Al-Mufradāt*, p. 531.

[89] *Tahrīr Alfāẓ al-Tanbīh*, p. 322.

you are conscious of Him, so that He is never forgotten, and that you thank Him, so that He is never shown ingratitude."[90] Yet other scholars of the past defined it to be, "It is that you worship Allāh, based upon light (i.e., knowledge) from Allāh, expecting the rewards from Allāh; and that you leave the prohibitions of Allāh, based upon light from Allāh, fearing the punishment of Allāh."

Therefore the essence of *taqwa* involves being conscious of Allāh, obeying His commandments, and avoiding His prohibitions. It involves constantly remembering Allāh, hoping for His mercy, and fearing His punishment.

The Proof that Taqwa is One of the Causes of Rizq

There are a number of evidences that show that *taqwa* is of the causes that increases a person's *rizq*.

Allāh states,

وَمَن يَتَّقِ ٱللَّهَ يَجْعَل لَّهُۥ مَخْرَجًا ﴿٢﴾ وَيَرْزُقْهُ
مِنْ حَيْثُ لَا يَحْتَسِبُ ۚ وَمَن يَتَوَكَّلْ عَلَى ٱللَّهِ فَهُوَ حَسْبُهُۥٓ ۚ إِنَّ ٱللَّهَ
بَٰلِغُ أَمْرِهِۦ ۚ قَدْ جَعَلَ ٱللَّهُ لِكُلِّ شَىْءٍ قَدْرًا ﴿٣﴾

> " ...And whosoever fears Allāh and keeps his duty to Him, He will make a way for him to get out (from every difficulty). And He will provide him from (sources) he never could imagine. And whosoever puts his trust in Allāh, then He will suffice him. Verily, Allāh will accomplish His purpose. Indeed Allāh has set a measure for all things." [Sūrah *al-Ṭalāq*, 2-3]

In these verses, Allāh clearly states that whoever has *taqwa* of Allāh will be graced with two blessings. Firstly, he will find a 'way out' of his problem. In other words, the constraint that he feels will be

---

[90] Reported by al-Māwardī in his *tafsīr* (2/248).

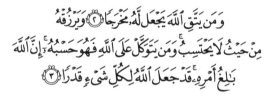

lifted, and his hardship will be replaced with ease. Secondly, he will be helped and aided from sources that he did not expect to be helped from. In other words, his *rizq* will come from sources that he least expected.

Ibn Kathīr stated, "This verse means that whoever fears Allāh concerning His commands (by performing them), and leaves His prohibitions, then Allāh will make an escape from his difficulty, and He will provide him sustenance (and aid) from sources that he did not expect, meaning that it never occurred to him that these sources could help him."[91]

How great and glorious this verse is! How optimistic it is! In this verse there is hope for those who have lost all hope, and there is a solution for those who felt there was none! This is why ʿAbdullāh ibn Masʿūd stated, "The greatest verse in the Qur'ān that provides an escape (from a difficult situation) is: 'Whoever fears Allāh, then He will make for him an escape.'"[92]

Another verse that proves that *taqwa* is one of the causes that increases *rizq* is the following verse:

وَلَوْ أَنَّ أَهْلَ ٱلْقُرَىٰٓ ءَامَنُوا۟ وَٱتَّقَوْا۟ لَفَتَحْنَا عَلَيْهِم بَرَكَـٰتٍ
مِّنَ ٱلسَّمَآءِ وَٱلْأَرْضِ وَلَـٰكِن كَذَّبُوا۟ فَأَخَذْنَـٰهُم بِمَا كَانُوا۟
يَكْسِبُونَ ﴿٩٦﴾

> "And if the people of the towns had believed and had *taqwa*, certainly, We would have opened for them blessings from the heaven and the earth, but they rejected (the Messengers). So We called them to task (with punishment) for what they used to earn." [Sūrah *al-Aʿrāf*, 96]

In this verse, Allāh states that if the people of the cities had only believed in Him, and had *taqwa*, then they would have been

---

[91] Ibn Kathīr (4/400).

[92] Reported by Ibn Kathīr (4/400).

blessed from the skies with rain, and from the earth with fruits and sustenance. Ibn ʿAbbās stated, "(This verse means that:) We would have increased our Provisions to them, and made every matter of theirs easy."[93]

This verse signifies that Allāh's blessings would be showered on them because of their faith and *taqwa*. This implies that these blessings would be pure and wholesome, with no evil effects, since their origin is from Allāh. Also, Allāh uses the plural: '...Our blessings...', showing that numerous blessings would descend upon them, not just one. In addition, Allāh states that these blessings would be '...from the skies and earth...', once again signifying the comprehensive nature of these blessings, for these are all the blessings one needs for this worldly life. The blessings from the skies include sending adequate rain – not too much nor too little – and ensuring that other environmental factors are suitable for life and harvest. The blessings from the earth include causing the crops to give their full produce, and the animals to reproduce and remain healthy, and peace and security to fill the land. In other words, the blessings from the skies and earth signifies that each and every blessing that is needed by them will be given to them.

Yet another verse that proves the importance of *taqwa* and its inducement of *rizq* occurs in reference to the Jews and Christians. Allāh states,

وَلَوْ أَنَّهُمْ أَقَامُوا
التَّوْرَىٰةَ وَالْإِنجِيلَ وَمَا أُنزِلَ إِلَيْهِم مِّن رَّبِّهِمْ لَأَكَلُوا مِن
فَوْقِهِمْ وَمِن تَحْتِ أَرْجُلِهِم ۚ مِّنْهُمْ أُمَّةٌ مُّقْتَصِدَةٌ ۖ وَكَثِيرٌ مِّنْهُمْ
سَاءَ مَا يَعْمَلُونَ ﴿٦٦﴾

[93] *Tafsīr Abī Saʿūd* (3/253).

"And if only they had acted according to the Torah, the Gospel, and what has (now) been sent down to them from their Lord (i.e., the Qur'ān), they would surely have received provision from above them and from underneath their feet. There are from amongst them people who are on the right course, but many of them do evil deeds." [Sūrah *al-Mā'idah*, 66]

In other words, if only the Jews and the Christians were to live by the laws that Allāh revealed to them – and this is the essence of *taqwa* – then Allāh would shower them with His blessings, to such an extent that they would eat from wherever and whatever they desired.

Imām al-Qurṭubī stated, "So Allāh has made *taqwa* a cause from the causes of *rizq*, as in these verses, and He has promised even more to those who thank Him, as He said, 'If you thank Me, then I will increase (your goods).'"[94]

Therefore, by leaving the *taqwa* of Allāh, one exposes himself to poverty:

ٱلشَّيْطَٰنُ يَعِدُكُمُ ٱلْفَقْرَ وَيَأْمُرُكُم بِٱلْفَحْشَآءِ
وَٱللَّهُ يَعِدُكُم مَّغْفِرَةً مِّنْهُ وَفَضْلًا ۗ وَٱللَّهُ وَٰسِعٌ عَلِيمٌ ﴿٢٦٨﴾

"*Shayṭān* threatens you with poverty and orders you to commit sins; whereas Allāh promises you forgiveness from Himself and Bounty, and Allāh is All-Sufficient for His creatures' needs, All-Knowing." [Sūrah *al-Baqarah*, 268]

ii. Seeking Forgiveness and Repentance

There is no doubt that one of the primary ways by which people can increase their *rizq* is to seek Allāh's forgiveness for their many sins. When people turn in repentance to Allāh, Allāh rewards them

---

[94] *Tafsīr al-Qurṭubī* (6/241).

by accepting their repentance, and by blessing them with worldly gain.

Before we bring forth the proofs for this, we must first define what proper repentance is.

The Meaning of Repentance

Many people erroneously believe that one must only say, "*Astaghfirullāh*" (I seek Allāh's forgiveness) in order for a person to repent. However, this is not the proper repentance that is praised in the Qur'ān and Sunnah. Such words, when uttered without any faith or effect on the heart, are signs of hypocrisy, and of the characteristics of liars.

The scholars of Islām have laid down certain conditions for any repentance to be accepted by Allāh.

The first and most important condition is that repentance be made purely for the sake of Allāh. No worldly factor should influence a person's motive for this religious act. The Prophet (ﷺ) said,

"All actions are (judged) by intentions."[95]

Therefore, even though a proper repentance causes one's *rizq* to increase (as we shall prove shortly), a person should not make this factor a *reason* for repentance. Rather, this blessing is one of the *products* of a true repentance, and therefore should not become the primary *motivation* for it. Secondly, the person should immediately stop performing the evil that he or she is doing. After all, how can the repentance be sincere if the person continues the sin while it is being repenting from? Thirdly, the person should make a sincere intention never to return to that sin. Fourthly, he should feel guilty over the sin that he has committed, for feeling a true sense

[95] Reported by al-Bukhārī (# 1) and others.

of shame and guilt is a part of repentance. Fifthly, one should seek Allāh's forgiveness, both verbally and by actions. Verbally, the one making repentance should pray that Allāh showers His Mercy and Forgiveness for the sins that have been committed. This can be done by any of the phrases that have been mentioned in the Qur'ān or Sunnah, the most common one being, "*Astaghfirullāh*."[96]

In actions, such a person should increase doing good deeds, in order to try to make up for the evil that was done. Lastly, if the sin involved taking the rights of other humans, or harming them in some way, then forgiveness must also be asked from those who have been wronged. The person who repents needs to make up to those that he or she has wronged. If some money was stolen, then it should be returned it to its proper owners. If someone had been slandered or backbitten, then that same person should be praised in the gatherings where he or she was previously slandered. Only when a person fulfils all of these conditions is the repentance proper and acceptable, and only then will it bring about the desired results.

One of the famous scholars of the Arabic language, Imām Rāghib al-Isfahānī, remarked, "Repentance in the *sharīʿah* is defined to be: leaving the sin due to its filthy nature, feeling guilty over the act that he has done, making a sincere intention never to return to that act, and trying to make up that act (by doing as many good deeds) as he can. Only when all four of these conditions are met will the repentance be acceptable."[97]

The Proof that Seeking Forgiveness Increases Rizq

There are a number of evidences found in the Qur'ān and sunnah that show that seeking forgiveness increases one's *rizq*. Some of these evidences are as follows:

---

[96] Meaning: I seek Allāh's forgiveness.

[97] *Mufradāt*, p. 76.

Allāh states in the Qur'ān that the Prophet Nūḥ said to his people,

فَقُلْتُ ٱسْتَغْفِرُوا۟ رَبَّكُمْ إِنَّهُۥ كَانَ غَفَّارًا ﴿١٠﴾
يُرْسِلِ ٱلسَّمَآءَ عَلَيْكُم مِّدْرَارًا ﴿١١﴾ وَيُمْدِدْكُم بِأَمْوَٰلٍ وَبَنِينَ وَيَجْعَل
لَّكُمْ جَنَّٰتٍ وَيَجْعَل لَّكُمْ أَنْهَٰرًا ﴿١٢﴾

> "I said (to them): 'Ask forgiveness from your Lord: Verily, He is Oft-Forgiving; He will (then) send rain to you in abundance, and give you increase in wealth and children, and bestow on you gardens, and bestow on you rivers.'" [Sūrah *Nūḥ*, 10-12]

This verse proves a number of points:

- That Allāh is the one that forgives sins. This is proven by Nūḥ's saying, "He is the one that continually forgives."
- That seeking forgiveness causes Allāh to bless the people by sending them rain, not just once, but continually, time after time. This is proven by the word, '...in abundance.'
- It also causes a person increase in money and children, since Allāh states that He would '...increase your wealth and sons.'
- It also causes a person to gain property and land, since Allāh says, '...and He will give you gardens...'
- Lastly, it also ensures the proper cultivation of those lands, as Allāh says, '...and He will give you rivers.'

Imam al-Qurṭubī stated, "In this verse, and also the verse in Sūrah *Hūd* (which will be discussed next), are clear proofs that asking for forgiveness is a cause of the descent of *rizq* and rain."[98]

---

[98] *Tafsīr al-Qurṭubi*, v. 18, p. 302.

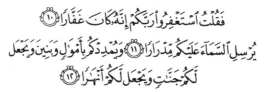

Al-Ḥāfiẓ Ibn Kathīr stated, "This verse means that if you repent to Allāh, and seek His forgiveness, and obey Him, then your *rizq* will increase, and you will be fed from the blessings of the skies (i.e., rain), and the fruits of the earth will grow for you, and the crops would grow, and the udder would be full, and He will give you property, wealth and children, and He will give you gardens of all types of fruit, and scatter therein running streams."[99]

This was why great scholars and leaders of the past used to seek Allāh's forgiveness at times of drought or poverty.

It is narrated once that 'Umar ibn al-Khaṭṭāb called the people together after they had been afflicted with a drought. Instead of praying a long rain prayer[100], he sought Allāh's forgiveness for their sins. When the people asked him concerning this, he recited,

يُرْسِلِ ٱلسَّمَآءَ عَلَيْكُم مِّدْرَارًا ﴿١١﴾

"He will send you rain to you in abundance." [Sūrah *Nūḥ*,11]

Likewise, a person came to al-Ḥasan al-Baṣrī, the famous Successor, and complained to him of drought. Ḥasan replied, "Seek Allāh's forgiveness."

A second man came to him, and asked him to pray that Allāh bless him with a child. Ḥasan said, "Seek Allāh's forgiveness."

Yet a third man came to him, and complained that his crop was not fruitful. Once again, Ḥasan said, "Seek Allāh's forgiveness."

One of his students said, "Different people came to you with different complaints, yet you ordered all of them to do the same thing: to seek Allāh's forgiveness!"

---

[99] *Tafsīr Ibn Kathīr*, v. 4, p. 449.

[100] There is a special type of prayer that the Prophet (ﷺ) encouraged the Muslims to perform at times of drought called *Ṣalāt al-Istisqā*.

Ḥasan replied, "I did not say anything from myself! Allāh has said in Sūrah *Nūḥ*,

فَقُلْتُ ٱسْتَغْفِرُوا۟ رَبَّكُمْ إِنَّهُۥ كَانَ غَفَّارًا ﴿١٠﴾
يُرْسِلِ ٱلسَّمَآءَ عَلَيْكُم مِّدْرَارًا ﴿١١﴾ وَيُمْدِدْكُم بِأَمْوَٰلٍ وَبَنِينَ وَيَجْعَل
لَّكُمْ جَنَّٰتٍ وَيَجْعَل لَّكُمْ أَنْهَٰرًا ﴿١٢﴾

"'I said (to them): 'Ask forgiveness from your Lord: Verily, He is Oft-Forgiving; He will send rain to you in abundance; and give you increase in wealth and children, and bestow on you gardens and bestow on you rivers.'" [Sūrah *Nūḥ*, 10-12][101]

Yet another proof that seeking forgiveness increases one's *rizq* is the advice that the Prophet Hūd gave to his people, which was similar to the advice of Prophet Nūḥ.

وَيَٰقَوْمِ ٱسْتَغْفِرُوا۟ رَبَّكُمْ ثُمَّ تُوبُوٓا۟ إِلَيْهِ يُرْسِلِ ٱلسَّمَآءَ
عَلَيْكُم مِّدْرَارًا وَيَزِدْكُمْ قُوَّةً إِلَىٰ قُوَّتِكُمْ وَلَا تَتَوَلَّوْا۟
مُجْرِمِينَ ﴿٥٢﴾

"And O my people! Ask forgiveness of your Lord and then repent to Him, He will send you (from the sky) abundant rain, and add strength to your strength, so do not turn away as evil-doers." [Sūrah *Hūd*; 52]

Ibn Kathīr said, commenting on this verse, "Then Hūd commanded them to seek forgiveness from their Lord, for in it is the removal of the past sins, and by repentance the sins to come also. And whoever has this characteristic, then Allāh will make his *rizq* easy to obtain, and make his affairs easy for him, and protect his interests. And this is why Allāh has said, "He will send the rains upon you continuously."

---

[101] *Tafsīr al-Qurṭubī*, (18/302).

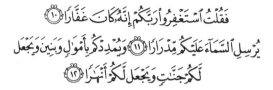

This concept is also mentioned in another verse in the Qur'ān. Allāh states,

وَأَنِ ٱسْتَغْفِرُوا۟
رَبَّكُمْ ثُمَّ تُوبُوٓا۟ إِلَيْهِ يُمَتِّعْكُم مَّتَٰعًا حَسَنًا إِلَىٰٓ أَجَلٍ مُّسَمًّى وَيُؤْتِ
كُلَّ ذِى فَضْلٍ فَضْلَهُۥ ۖ وَإِن تَوَلَّوْا۟ فَإِنِّىٓ أَخَافُ عَلَيْكُمْ عَذَابَ يَوْمٍ
كَبِيرٍ ﴿٣﴾

> "And seek the forgiveness of your Lord, and turn to Him in repentance, that He may grant you good enjoyment, for a term appointed, and bestow His abounding grace to every owner of grace. But if you turn away, then I fear for you the torment of a Great Day." [Sūrah *Hūd*, 3]

This verse has been phrased very eloquently, for it has been expressed as a condition and a response to that condition. The great scholar Muḥammad al-Amīn al-Shanqīṭī stated, "This beautiful verse proves that seeking forgiveness from Allāh, and turning to Him in repentance, is of the causes of Allāh showering His blessings upon the one who does these things, because it has been phrased as a condition and a response to that condition."

Imām al-Qurṭubī wrote, "This is indeed the fruits of seeking forgiveness. For He will provide you of all types of ease and comfort, of increased *rizq* and easy living. And He will not destroy you like He did those before you."[102]

Yet another evidence that proves that seeking forgiveness and repentance opens the doors of sustenance is the ḥadīth that mentions that the Prophet (ﷺ) said,

> "Whoever persists in asking forgiveness, Allāh will make for him, for every grief, a way out, and for every difficult situation,

---

[102] *Tafsīr al-Qurṭubī*, (9/403).

an exit, and He will provide him with sustenance from places that he did not expect."[103]

So in this ḥadīth, we learn three great blessings of repentance. And of these blessings is the fact that Allāh will provide people with help, money, and sustenance, from places and sources and means that they did not expect to receive them from! What a great blessing, and what a beautiful reward, for the one who seeks forgiveness for his own sins! But beware of seeking forgiveness with the tongue without sincerity, for such a repentance is not a true repentance.

iii. Putting One's Trust in Allāh

One of the factors that causes *rizq* to increase is when people put their trust in Allāh, realizing that nothing occurs except with the will of Allāh, and whatever occurs, occurs because of Divine Wisdom. The believer accepts the Will of Allāh, without getting angry or questioning His Will. The believer realizes that Allāh has indeed decided what is best, and has full faith in whatever Allāh decrees for him.

So what is the true meaning of *tawakkul*, of putting one's trust in Allāh? And what is the proof that *tawakkul* increases one's *rizq*?

---

[103] Reported in *Sunan Abī Dāwūd,* (# 1515), *Musnad Aḥmad*, (# 2234), and others. This ḥadīth has been declared authentic (*Ṣaḥīḥ*) by al-Ḥākim in his *Mustadrak* (4/262), al-Suyūṭi in his *al-Jāmiʿ*, and Aḥmad Shākir (in the footnotes of his editing of the *Musnad*, 4/55). However, al-Dhahabī in his checking of al-Ḥakim's *Mustadrak* (4/262) pointed out that it has al-Ḥakam ibn Musʿab in its chain, and he is unknown. Because of this reason, Shaykh al-Albānī declared the ḥadīth to be weak (see *Ḍaʿīf Sunan Abī Dāwūd*, p. 149, and *al-Silsilah al-Ḍaʿīfah,* # 705). In either case, the verses of the Qur'ān that have preceded this ḥadīth are sufficient as evidence for this point.

The True Meaning of Tawakkul

The topic of *tawakkul* is very important and frequently misunderstood. Briefly put, the essence of *tawakkul* involves attaching one's heart to Allāh, and resigning one's fate to Allāh. The person with *tawakkul* realizes that there is no power to obtain good, or avert evil, except with Allāh, and all blessings and tribulations are the result of Allāh's decree.

It is imperative that a person realizes that true *tawakkul* does not mean leaving the actions that are necessary to achieve one's goal. On the contrary, true *tawakkul necessitates* that a person strive, with all efforts and in all permissible ways, to achieve what is desired, all the while realizing that such efforts will not procure the desired results unless Allāh has already willed it. True *tawakkul* does not mean being lazy, or not taking the necessary precautions.

A Bedouin came to the Prophet (ﷺ) and asked, "Should I tie my camel up (to prevent it from running away), or should I put my trust in Allāh?"

This Bedouin thought – as many ignorant Muslims of our time still do – that *tawakkul* meant leaving the necessary precautions, and not doing one's best to achieve the desired goal. But the Prophet (ﷺ) informed him of the true nature of *tawakkul*. He replied,

"Tie it up, then put your trust (in Allāh)!"[104]

This ḥadīth is clear proof that true *tawakkul* is a matter of the heart. It does not negate bodily actions to achieve the desired ends. On the contrary, true *tawakkul* necessitates these actions, because the believer realizes that the one who has created the object has also created the means to obtain that object. Therefore, the believer desires that object, and strives by all allowable means to obtain it,

[104] Reported by Ibn Ḥibbān in his *Ṣaḥīḥ* (# 731 of the *Iḥsān* edition), and al-Ḥākim in his *Mustadrak* (3/623), where al-Dhahabī said of it, "Its chain of narrators is strong."

but fully realizes that success, or otherwise, is up to the Will of Allāh.

The Proof that Tawakkul is a Means of Rizq

ʿUmar ibn al-Khaṭṭāb reported that the Prophet (ﷺ) said,

> "If you were to put your trust in Allāh (*tawakkul*) the way that Allāh deserves, then you would be provided for as the birds are; they leave (in search of food) at the beginning of the day famished, and they return at the end of the day full."[105]

This beautiful ḥadīth describes the phenomenon of one of the creatures that Allāh has created, and its strange cycle. Every day it leaves its nest in the morning, in search of food, and every day it returns at night, having succeeded in its quest. The true believers who put their trust in Allāh are reminded that they will likewise be rewarded. Such a believer will taste the fruits of his trust, and how can he not, when the One that he trusted was the Ever-Living who never dies? Allāh says,

وَتَوَكَّلْ عَلَى ٱلْحَيِّ ٱلَّذِى لَا يَمُوتُ

> "So put your trust (*tawakkul*) in the one that is Ever-Living, the One who does not die." [Sūrah *al-Furqān*, 58]

Allāh also says,

وَيَرْزُقْهُ
مِنْ حَيْثُ لَا يَحْتَسِبُ وَمَن يَتَوَكَّلْ عَلَى ٱللَّهِ فَهُوَ حَسْبُهُۥٓ إِنَّ ٱللَّهَ
بَٰلِغُ أَمْرِهِۦ قَدْ جَعَلَ ٱللَّهُ لِكُلِّ شَىْءٍ قَدْرًا ﴿٣﴾

[105] Reported by al-Tirmidhī in his *Sunan* (# 2447), Ibn Mājah (# 4216), Aḥmad in his *Musnad* (# 205), Ibn Ḥibbān in his *Ṣaḥīḥ* (# 559 of the edited *Iḥsān*), al-Ḥākim in his *Mustadrak* (4/318), and others. It was declared authentic by al-Tirmidhī, al-Ḥākim, al-Dhahabī, Aḥmad Shākir, and al-Albānī (see *al-Silsilat al-Ṣaḥīḥah,* #310).

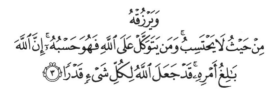

> "And He will provide him from (sources) he never could imagine. And whosoever puts his trust (*tawakkul*) in Allāh, then He will suffice him. Verily, Allāh will accomplish his purpose. Indeed Allāh has set a measure for all things." [Sūrah *al-Ṭalāq*, 3]

Have you not read the promise of Allāh:

وَإِنْ خِفْتُمْ عَيْلَةً فَسَوْفَ يُغْنِيكُمُ ٱللَّهُ مِن فَضْلِهِۦٓ إِن
شَآءَ ۚ إِنَّ ٱللَّهَ عَلِيمٌ حَكِيمٌ ﴿٢٨﴾

> "If you fear poverty, Allāh will enrich you if He wills, out of His Bounty. Surely, Allāh is All-Knowing, All-Wise?" [Sūrah *al-Tawbah*, 28]

Therefore, O Believer, do not be like the hypocrites who were not satisfied with whatever Allāh gave them; rather, put your trust in Allāh, then and only then Allāh will give you more:

وَلَوْ أَنَّهُمْ رَضُوا۟ مَآ ءَاتَىٰهُمُ ٱللَّهُ
وَرَسُولُهُۥ وَقَالُوا۟ حَسْبُنَا ٱللَّهُ سَيُؤْتِينَا ٱللَّهُ مِن فَضْلِهِۦ
وَرَسُولُهُۥٓ إِنَّآ إِلَى ٱللَّهِ رَٰغِبُونَ ﴿٥٩﴾

> "If only they (the hypocrites) had been satisfied with what Allāh and His Messenger gave them and had said: 'Allāh is Sufficient for us. Allāh will give us of His Bounty, and (also) His Messenger, we implore Allāh (to enrich us).'" [Sūrah *al-Tawbah*, 59]

In the ḥadīth of 'Umar above, the true meaning of *tawakkul* is also re-enforced. The Prophet (ﷺ) described this bird as one who leaves in the early parts of the day, in search for food. It does not remain in its nest, believing that food will come to it, but rather strives to achieve the desired goal. It prepares itself early in the morning, leaving its comfortable nest in search of food. And then, and only then, does it arrive at dusk, tired, yet with a full stomach.

And so too is the example of the true believer who strives in order to earn the desired *rizq*, and then places *tawakkul* in Allāh.

iv. Constantly Worshipping Allāh

Of the many ways that people can be blessed by Allāh in their worldly affairs is by constantly worshipping Allāh, striving for the Hereafter. But does this imply that a person stays in the *masjid* all day, and prays all night, leaving one's duties towards one's family and business? And what is the proof that worshipping Allāh increases one's *rizq*?

The Meaning of 'Constant Worship'

Let it not be assumed that the meaning of this phrase is to leave worldly affairs, and abandon all worldly efforts. What is meant is that a person is always conscious of his or her worship. The true believer does not let family or business come in the way of worship. During the acts of worship, such a believer is humble and attentive to the worship, realizing the greatness of the One that is being worshipped. The mind of the true believer does not wander to other thoughts, of worldly affairs, and business, and family, and other matters. It is as if, like the Prophet (ﷺ) said, he

> '...worships Allāh as though you see Him, for even if you do not see Him, of a surety He sees you.'[106]

And during the acts of daily life, the believer remembers Allāh always, and strives to please Him by obeying His commandments and staying away from His prohibitions. So such a person is kind to family and honest to customers, conscious that all deeds are being monitored by Allāh. This is the meaning of 'constant worship.'

And realize that the concept of worship in Islām is not limited to a few physical acts, such as prostration, and recitation. Rather,

---

[106] Part of the ḥadith of Jibrīl, reported by Muslim (# 1), and others.

every single act, if done for the sake of Allāh, becomes an act of worship. Thus, when a person leaves his home, intending to earn some money with which he can feed his family, then this is an act of worship. When he studies a profession, intending to earn a *ḥalāl* income, then this studying becomes an act of worship. When a mother takes care of her household, intending to please her husband and raise their children as strong, pious Muslims, then her cooking and cleaning become acts of worship. When a person eats food, intending to gain strength to do deeds pleasing to Allāh, then this is in act of worship. Even when one satisfies his or her sexual desires with one's spouse, intending purity and avoiding illegal means of satisfaction, then this act too becomes an act of worship.

The Proof that Constant Worship Increases Rizq

There are a number of evidences that prove that a person who constantly worships Allāh will be blessed with contentment and *rizq*.

Abū Hurayrah stated that the Prophet (ﷺ) said,

> "Allāh says, 'O Son of Ādam! Take time out to constantly worship me, I will fill your chest with richness, and remove your poverty. And if you do not do so, I will make your hands filled with occupation, and will not remove your poverty."[107]

In this ḥadīth *Qudsī*,[108] Allāh informs us that those who worship Him constantly will be rewarded by having their hearts filled with richness, and their poverty covered up. This indicates that such people will not be dependant on others to supply their needs; rather, Allāh will cover up their condition, and supply them with *rizq* without having to go to other people to obtain it.

---

[107] Reported by al-Tirmidhī (# 2583), Ibn Mājah (# 4159) and others. Al-Albānī declared it to be authentic in his *Ṣaḥīḥ Sunan al-Tirmidhī*, (2/300).

[108] A ḥadith *qudsī* is one in which the Prophet (ﷺ) narrates from Allāh.

On the other hand, if a person does not take the time out to worship Allāh, Allāh will punish him by making him very busy, or, as the wording in the ḥadīth states, '…fill your hands with chores…', meaning that he will constantly be working. Yet, despite all this hard work, because this work is deprived of Allāh's blessings, he will not be able to cover up his poverty, and will still be dependant on people.

So ponder, O Muslim, over this ḥadīth, and see for yourself if the statement of the Prophet (ﷺ) is true! Look around you, and observe how many are the seekers of this world who work day and night, yet, because they do not take the time out to worship Allāh, their efforts are of no use to them. Instead of making themselves richer and richer, their lives become busier and busier, their work increases, and they burden themselves with debt upon debt. If only these people realised that the solution to their problems is not to leave the worship of Allāh, but rather to turn to Allāh, and take the time out of their 'busy' schedule to worship Him – if only they realised this, then their results would have been fruitful. Instead of feeling the constraint and confinement of the heart, Allāh would have made them feel rich and free. Instead of remaining busy, and increasing their debts, Allāh would have lessened their daily load, and covered up their poverty! But alas! These misguided souls were deceived into thinking that, in order to increase their wealth, they would have to work all day long for it. To such misguided souls, the worship of Allāh was a hindrance in their work; it was an impediment in their daily schedule, and so they lost the good of this life and the Hereafter!

In a similar narration to the above ḥadīth, Ma'qal ibn Yasār reported that the Prophet (ﷺ) said,

> "Your Lord, all glory and honour be to Him, says, 'O Son of Ādam! Take the time out to constantly worship Me, I will fill your chest with richness! O Son of Ādam! Do not distance

> yourself from Me, or I will fill your chest with poverty, and fill your hands with work!'"[109]

In this ḥadīth there is a powerful reminder that true richness is a blessing that is bestowed by Allāh to the believers, and comprises a peace and contentment of the heart. The rich people are those who feel content with what Allāh has bestowed upon them, even if others perceive it as little. And the poor person is the one who is greedy for the possessions in other people's hands, even if perceived by others to be wealthy!

Yet another reminder in this ḥadīth is that people's efforts in obtaining wealth are not necessarily proportional to the amount of wealth acquired. Rather, if people take time out of their daily schedules to worship Allāh, and make sure that their pursuit of *rizq* does not distract them from the remembrance of Allāh, then they will *insha-Allāh* obtain more *rizq* than those who spend all of their time away from the worship of Allāh.

Another narration also proves that the constant worship of Allāh increases one's *rizq*. Ubayy ibn Ka'ab asked the Prophet (ﷺ), "O Messenger of Allāh! I frequently send salutations upon you, so how much of my prayer should be upon you (i.e., how much of my *dhikr* should be spent upon sending salutations upon you)?" The Prophet (ﷺ) replied,

> "As much as you want."

So he said, "A fourth?" The Prophet (ﷺ) replied,

> "As much as you wish, and if you increase, it is for your own good."

So he said, "Half?" The Prophet (ﷺ) replied,

> "As much as you wish, and if you increase, it is for your own good."

---

[109] It was reported by al-Ḥākim in his *Mustadrak* (4/326) who said of it, "This is a ḥadīth with an authentic *isnād*," and al-Dhahabī agreed with him, as did al-Albānī in his *Ṣaḥīḥah* (# 1359).

So he said, "Two-thirds?" The Prophet (ﷺ) replied,

> "As much as you wish, and if you increase, it is for your own good."

Then he replied, "I will make my entire prayers for you (i.e., in sending salutations upon you)." So the Prophet (ﷺ) replied,

> "In that case, your troubles will be taken care of, and your sins forgiven."[110]

In this ḥadīth, the Prophet (ﷺ) informed us that those who continually send their *salāms* upon him (ﷺ) – the sending of which is one of the most noble acts of worship – will have all of their troubles, financial or otherwise, taken care of.

v. Thanking Allāh

One of the means through which people are guaranteed an increase in the blessings bestowed upon them by Allāh is the continual thanking of Allāh for the present blessings that they have. When people are grateful for the blessings that Allāh gives them, Allāh then increases these blessings.

The Proof that Thanking Allāh Increases One's Rizq

Allāh states,

وَإِذْ تَأَذَّنَ
رَبُّكُمْ لَئِن شَكَرْتُمْ لَأَزِيدَنَّكُمْ وَلَئِن كَفَرْتُمْ إِنَّ
عَذَابِي لَشَدِيدٌ ﴿٧﴾

---

[110] Reported by al-Tirmidhī (# 2457) who said it is *ḥasan Ṣaḥīḥ*; ʿAbd ibn Ḥumayd in his *Musnad* (# 170 of *al-Muntakhab*); Ibn Abī Shaybah in his *al-Muṣannaf* (# 8706); al-Bayhaqī in his *Shuʿab al-Īmān* (# 1748) and others, with similar wordings and various chains, all of which clearly make the ḥadīth *ḥasan*, as is the opinion of Ibn al-Qayyim in his *Jalā al-Afhām* (p. 150).

"And (remember) when your Lord proclaimed: 'If you are thankful, I will give you more (of My Blessings), but if you are thankless (i.e., disbelievers), then verily, My punishment is indeed severe.'" [Sūrah *Ibrāhīm*, 7]

This is a clear, explicit verse in which Allāh promises an increase in blessings if His servants are thankful to Him.

This is one of the reasons that we find that the Prophet (ﷺ) would continually thank Allāh, for it is only befitting that the One who provides all that we have be thanked. The prophets before us even asked Allāh to help them in this noble undertaking, for, as Sulaymān prayed,

فَتَبَسَّمَ ضَاحِكًا مِّن قَوْلِهَا وَقَالَ رَبِّ أَوْزِعْنِىٓ أَنْ أَشْكُرَ نِعْمَتَكَ ٱلَّتِىٓ أَنْعَمْتَ عَلَىَّ وَعَلَىٰ وَٰلِدَىَّ وَأَنْ أَعْمَلَ صَٰلِحًا تَرْضَىٰهُ وَأَدْخِلْنِى بِرَحْمَتِكَ فِى عِبَادِكَ ٱلصَّٰلِحِينَ ﴿١٩﴾

"So he (Sulaymān) smiled, amused at her speech (i.e., the speech of the ant) and said: 'My Lord! Inspire (and bestow) upon me the power (and ability) that I may be grateful for Your Favours which You have bestowed upon me, and upon my parents, and that I may do righteous good deeds that will please You, and admit me by Your Mercy among Your righteous slaves." [Sūrah *al-Naml*, 19]

Likewise, the Muslim is commanded by Allāh,

رَبِّ أَوْزِعْنِىٓ أَنْ أَشْكُرَ نِعْمَتَكَ ٱلَّتِىٓ أَنْعَمْتَ عَلَىَّ وَعَلَىٰ وَٰلِدَىَّ وَأَنْ أَعْمَلَ صَٰلِحًا تَرْضَىٰهُ وَأَصْلِحْ لِى فِى ذُرِّيَّتِىٓ ۖ إِنِّى تُبْتُ إِلَيْكَ وَإِنِّى مِنَ ٱلْمُسْلِمِينَ ﴿١٥﴾

"... 'My Lord! Grant me the power (and ability) that I may be grateful for Your Favours which You have bestowed upon me and upon my parents, and that I may do righteous good deeds, such as please You and make my off-spring good. Truly, I have turned to You in repentance, and truly, I am one of the Muslims (submitting to Your will)." [Sūrah *al-Aḥqāf*, 15]

The believer thanks Allāh, by praising Him, attributing all of his blessings to Him, and worshipping Him.

So by thanking Allāh for the good that a believer has been blessed with, he is guaranteed an increase in these goods.

vi. Frequently Performing *Ḥajj* and *ʿUmrah*

Of the greatest blessings of Allāh, and of the easiest ways to increase one's *rizq*, is the frequent performance of *Ḥajj* and *ʿUmrah*. When a person takes the time and effort to travel to Makkah, and spends of his wealth for the pleasure of Allāh, then Allāh rewards him by increasing his *rizq*.

The Proof that the Performance of Ḥajj and ʿUmrah Increases Rizq

It has been reported by ʿAbdullāh ibn Masʿūd that the Prophet (ﷺ) said,

> "Follow up between *Ḥajj* and *ʿUmrah* (i.e., continually repeat the performance of *Ḥajj* and *ʿUmrah*), because they both eliminate poverty and sins just like a furnace eliminates the dirty impurities of iron, gold and silver. And an accepted *Ḥajj* has no reward less than paradise!"[111]

In this beautiful ḥadīth, the Prophet (ﷺ) encouraged the Muslims to follow up one *Ḥajj* after another, and one *ʿUmrah* after another, for the rewards of this small deed are great. Not only

---

[111] Reported by al-Tirmidhī in his *Sunan* (# 807), al-Nasāʾī (5/115), Aḥmad in his *Musnad* (# 3669), and others. It was authenticated by al-Tirmidhī, Aḥmad Shākir, and al-Albānī in his *Ṣaḥīḥ Sunan al-Tirmidhī* (1/245). This exact same ḥadīth, without the last sentence, was also reported by Ibn ʿAbbās in *Sunan al-Nasāʾī* (5/115).

will a person increase his *rizq*, he will also have his sins removed, just like a burning furnace refines iron, gold and silver from impurities!

vii. Establishing the Ties of Kinship

Of the established and proven methods to increase one's *rizq* is to establish the ties of kinship. Therefore, it is essential to discuss three topics. Firstly, the people that are considered one's 'kin'. Secondly, the evidences that prove the fact that establishing one's kinship increases one's *rizq*. Thirdly, the proper manner of establishing the ties of kinship.

The Meaning of 'Establishing the Ties of Kinship'

A person's 'kinship' are his or her relatives. It does not matter if these relatives will inherit from this person or not, or whether they fall within the prohibited categories of marriage (*maḥārim*) or not. All of a person's close relatives, from both mother's and father's side, are considered to be 'kin'. So, a person's maternal and paternal uncles, maternal and paternal aunts, their children, their father's maternal and paternal uncles and aunts, their mother's maternal and paternal uncles and aunts, their children, etc., are all considered relatives.

The 'establishment' of the ties of kinship means showing these relatives kindness, compassion, and mercy. It necessitates keeping in touch with them, paying them visits, and inquiring about their health and welfare. It obligates helping them out in whatever way possible, to the best of one's means.

The closer and stronger the relationship is, the more important it becomes to establish these ties. Thus, a brother or sister has a much greater right than does a cousin. Likewise, a 'close' (first) cousin has a greater right than a 'distant' (second or third) cousin, and so forth. So the exact manners of establishing these ties is proportional to the strength of relationship that exists between them; the closer the relationship, the more that needs to be done, and *vice versa*.

The Proof that this Establishment Increases Rizq

There are a number of references in the ḥadīths of the Prophet (ﷺ) to the effect that establishing the ties of kinship increases a person's *rizq*.

Abū Hurayrah reported that the Prophet (ﷺ) said,

> "Whoever is pleased with the fact that his *rizq* be increased, and his life-span be extended[112], then let him establish the ties of kinship."[113]

In another narration reported by Anas ibn Mālik, the Prophet (ﷺ) said,

> "Whoever wishes to have his *rizq* increased, and his life-span be extended, then let him establish the ties of kinship."[114]

---

[112] A person might ask, "How can one's life-span be extended, when Allāh has already stated in the Qur'ān that a person can never change the time of his death. What is the interpretation of this ḥadīth?" The answer to this question is that the scholars of ḥadīth have interpreted this ḥadīth in one of two ways. It could be that what is implied in the ḥadīth is that the blessings of a person's life will increase, in that he will be able to do more in a shorter period of time, as if he had lived longer. Another interpretation is that the ḥadīth is to be taken at face value, and that a person's life-span literally increases. However, Allāh has already decreed this increase. So, it is possible that Allāh has decreed that the life-span of so-and-so will be sixty years if he does not fulfil the ties of kinship, and seventy years if he does. Now, the angel of death that had been assigned to him does not know how long he will live, but Allāh already knows whether this man will establish the ties of kinship or not. If he does not, then he will die sooner, whereas if he does, then his life-span will be 'extended' by the Will and Knowledge of Allāh.

[113] Reported by al-Bukhārī (#5985), and others.

[114] Reported by al-Bukhārī (# 5986) and others.

Abū Hurayrah also reported that the Prophet (ﷺ) said,

> "Learn (enough) of your lineage, so that you can establish the ties of kinship, for establishing the ties of kinship increases the love amongst the families, and multiplies wealth, and extends age."[115]

ʿAlī ibn Abī Ṭālib reported that the Prophet (ﷺ) said,

> "Whoever is pleased to have his life extended, and his *rizq* increased, and an evil death be averted from him, then let him have *taqwa* of Allāh, and let him fulfil the ties of kinship!"[116]

Look at this beautiful ḥadīth, and what it describes of good! Who is there who does not wish to have his life extended? And who is there that does not wish to increase his money and wealth? And who is there who does not wish to save himself from an evil and humiliating death? And here the Prophet (ﷺ), the truthful, has informed us that whoever possesses two characteristics will be able to obtain all of these blessings. These two characteristics are simple and easy, but only for those who sincerely desire the rewards of Allāh. These two characteristics are: *taqwa* of Allāh, and fulfilling the ties of kinship. This is why ʿAbdullāh ibn ʿUmar, the famous companion of the Prophet (ﷺ), stated,

> "Whoever has *taqwa* of his Lord, and establishes the ties of kinship, will have his life extended, and his money increased, and his family will love him."[117]

In fact, so great and blessed is the act of fulfilling the ties of kinship, that it is possible that even an evil person can taste the

---

[115] Reported by al-Tirmidhī (# 2045), and Aḥmad (# 8855). It was authenticated by al-Ḥākim in his *Mustadrak* (6/96), and al-Dhahabī agreed with him. Likewise Aḥmad Shākir and al-Albānī graded it to be authentic (see *Ṣaḥīḥ Sunan al-Tirmidhī*, 2/190).

[116] Reported by Ahmad in his *Musnad* (# 1212), and Ahmad Shākir said of it, "Its chain is authentic" (2/290 of his edition).

[117] Reported by Imām al-Bukhārī in his book *al-Adab al-Mufrad* (# 59).

fruits of this noble task. Abū Bakrah reported that the Prophet (ﷺ) said,

> "The swiftest of good deeds in retribution is the (act of) fulfilling the ties of kinship. So much so, that it is possible that a family can be evil, but their money and their numbers will increase if they fulfil the ties of kinship. And there is no family that fulfils the ties of kinship that is needy (of other people.)"[118]

What great rewards must exist in fulfilling the ties of kinship, when even evil people – those who neither fear Allāh nor worship Him properly – can taste the rewards of this act! And imagine how much greater the rewards will be, when this act is done by one who fears Allāh, and loves Him, and strives his best to obey Him. Indeed, fulfilling the ties of kinship is one of the easiest and most blessed way to increase one's life and wealth.

The Proper Manner to Establish the Ties of Kinship

Earlier, it was mentioned that the responsibility of each relationship is based on the strength of the bonds that bind individuals together. Of primary importance are, of course, the mother and father. Concerning the parents and their rights in Islām, the Qur'ān lays down clear guidelines:

۞ وَقَضَىٰ رَبُّكَ أَلَّا تَعْبُدُوٓاْ إِلَّآ إِيَّاهُ وَبِٱلْوَٰلِدَيْنِ إِحْسَٰنًا ۚ إِمَّا
يَبْلُغَنَّ عِندَكَ ٱلْكِبَرَ أَحَدُهُمَآ أَوْ كِلَاهُمَا فَلَا تَقُل لَّهُمَآ
أُفٍّ وَلَا تَنْهَرْهُمَا وَقُل لَّهُمَا قَوْلًا كَرِيمًا ﴿٢٣﴾

> "And your Lord has decreed that you worship none but Him, and that you be dutiful to your parents. If one of them or both of them attain old age in your life, say not to them a word of

[118] Reported by Ibn Hibbān in his *Ṣaḥīḥ* (# 440 of the *Iḥsān* edition), and it was authenticated by Shu'ayb al-'Arnā'ūṭ.

> disrespect, nor speak harshly to them, but address them in terms of honour." [Sūrah *al-Isrā*, 23]

The rights of the parents are followed by the rights of one's brothers and sisters, spouses and children, and uncles and aunts. Likewise, cousins, whether close or extended, also have a right of good treatment, and the strength of this relationship is proportional to the strength of the blood-relationship. So, for distant cousins, it might be sufficient to remain in contact with them, visit them occasionally (especially on important occasions, such as a marriage or death), and invite them over occasionally as well. If a person increases this, then it is more rewarding for him. For brothers and sisters, however, the relationship must be much stronger than this. One must look after their needs to the best of one's capabilities, inquire about their health and well-being, show concern for them, and so forth. Basically, Muslims should help out their relatives to the best of their abilities, in any manner that they can. Likewise, they should help out 'closer' relatives before 'distant' ones. So, a person's spouse and children have more of a right than uncles and aunts, and they in turn have more right than cousins, and so forth. Ibn Abī Jamrah stated, "Establishing the ties of kinship is done by (spending) money (on them), by helping them in their affairs, by repelling evil from them, by being nice to them, and by praying for them."

Many people mistakenly believe that fulfilling the ties of kinship implies being good to one's relatives in a worldly sense only. Therefore, if a close relative of theirs is doing a major sin, they will ignore this act, not give any advice to that relative, and meet and interact with such a relative as if he or she is a pious person. However, this is not what Islām asks. Islām demands that a person love and hate for the sake of Allāh. If a person is doing some evil, then it becomes the duty of every Muslim, especially his or her relatives, to advise this person and try their best to correct him. If a person feels that, by cutting ties with a certain individual, he will cause that individual to leave the sin that he is doing, then in this case to cut ties with him is in fact the proper way to fulfil the ties of kinship.

A person must look at the net result of what he or she will do, and judge accordingly. If there is a relative that is involved with some major sin or innovation, then it becomes obligatory to try to correct that person to the best of one's capabilities, and doing this is in fact 'establishing' the ties of kinship. Allāh says,

لَّا تَجِدُ قَوْمًا يُؤْمِنُونَ بِاللَّهِ وَالْيَوْمِ الْآخِرِ يُوَآدُّونَ مَنْ حَآدَّ اللَّهَ وَرَسُولَهُ وَلَوْ كَانُوٓا ءَابَآءَهُمْ أَوْ أَبْنَآءَهُمْ أَوْ إِخْوَٰنَهُمْ أَوْ عَشِيرَتَهُمْ أُوْلَٰٓئِكَ كَتَبَ فِى قُلُوبِهِمُ الْإِيمَٰنَ وَأَيَّدَهُم بِرُوحٍ مِّنْهُ وَيُدْخِلُهُمْ جَنَّٰتٍ تَجْرِى مِن تَحْتِهَا الْأَنْهَٰرُ خَٰلِدِينَ فِيهَا رَضِىَ اللَّهُ عَنْهُمْ وَرَضُوا۟ عَنْهُ أُوْلَٰٓئِكَ حِزْبُ اللَّهِ أَلَآ إِنَّ حِزْبَ اللَّهِ هُمُ الْمُفْلِحُونَ ﴿٢٢﴾

> "You will not find any people who believe in Allāh and the Last Day, making friendship with those who oppose Allāh and His Messenger, even though they were their fathers, or their sons, or their brothers, or their kindred (people). For such He has written Faith in their hearts and strengthened them with proofs from Him. And We will admit them to Gardens (Paradise) under which rivers flow, to dwell therein (forever). Allāh is pleased with them, and they with Him. They are the Party of Allāh. Verily, it is the Party of Allāh that will be successful." [Sūrah al-Mujādilah, 22]

This clearly shows that love for Allāh, and love for those who disbelieve and disobey Allāh, do not combine in the heart of one individual.

This does not, of course, mean that a person should not show kindness to his relatives if they are not Muslims. It does mean, though, that the primary reason for showing them kindness is to guide them to Islām. Again, a person must use his or her better judgement to decide a specific course of action. A certain person might feel that if he were to tell his sinning brother, "I will not visit your house or concern myself with your affairs, because you are a habitual drinker, and until you stop drinking, I will have no contact with you," then his brother will change his ways, and leave drinking. On the other hand, another person might feel that the best way to stop his brother would be to constantly call him up and visit him, in order to advise him to fear Allāh and leave drinking. Both of these people will be rewarded for 'establishing' the ties of kinship, because the purpose of both of these people was to try to correct their brother.

Ibn Abī Jamrah stated, "If the relatives are disbelievers, or evil sinners, then to cut all ties with them for the sake of Allāh is in fact 'establishing' the ties of kinship with them, with the condition that a person tried his best to advise them; then, if they persisted in their acts, to inform them that (his cutting of ties with them) is due to the fact that they have rejected the truth. However, this (cutting off) does not remove the obligation to fulfil the ties of kinship by praying for them in private that they return to the Straight Path."[119]

viii. Spending in the way of Allāh

Of the ways to increase a person's *rizq* is by spending in the way of Allāh.

The Meaning of 'Spending in the Way of Allāh'

There are three primary types of charity in Islām. Two of them are obligatory (with certain conditions), and one is voluntary. The two obligatory types are *zakāt* (which is given on certain types of livestock, agricultural produce, money, and business items),

---

[119] Taken from *Tuḥfah al-Aḥwadhī*, 6/30.

and *zakāt al-fiṭr* (which is given at the end of Ramaḍān as an expiation for any sins committed while fasting). The details for these two types of *zakāt* are found in the books of *fiqh*. The third type of charity is voluntary, and is known as *ṣadaqah*. *Ṣadaqah* is encouraged at all times and places.

All of these three types of charities come under 'spending' in the way of Allāh. So, whether a person pays *zakāt* to the poor, or helps build a *masjid*, or supports an Islāmic school, or takes responsibility for the welfare of orphans, widows, or students of knowledge, all of these noble tasks will bring the desired reward. The point is that a person should spend of his wealth on causes that are pleasing to Allāh.

The Proof that Spending in the Way of Allāh Increases Sustenance

There are numerous evidences in the Qur'ān and sunnah which prove that spending in the way of Allāh is a direct cause for being blessed with extra sustenance. Of these evidence are the following.

Allāh says in the Qur'ān,

قُلْ
إِنَّ رَبِّي يَبْسُطُ ٱلرِّزْقَ لِمَن يَشَآءُ مِنْ عِبَادِهِۦ وَيَقْدِرُ لَهُۥٓ ۚ وَمَآ
أَنفَقْتُم مِّن شَىْءٍ فَهُوَ يُخْلِفُهُۥ ۖ وَهُوَ خَيْرُ ٱلرَّٰزِقِينَ ﴿٣٩﴾

> "Say: Truly, my Lord enlarges the provision for whom He wills of His slaves, and (also) restricts (it) for him, and whatever you spend of anything (in Allāh's cause), He will replace it. And He is the Best of providers." [Sūrah *Saba'*, 39]

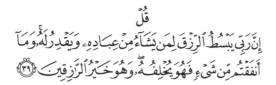

Ibn Kathīr commented on this verse, saying, "Meaning that no matter how much you spend, on matters that He has made obligatory upon you, and (on matters) that are permissible, Allāh will replace it in this world with a substitute (meaning more money), and in the Hereafter with rewards, as has been explained in the sunnah."[120]

Therefore, this verse shows that whoever spends in the way of Allāh has qualified to be of those whose money will be substituted for other money. The implication of this is that he who does not spend in the way of Allāh has not qualified for this blessing, hence his money will of a surety continually decrease.

In fact, the Arabic phrasing of this verse contains three separate means of emphasizing this fact. Firstly, it appears in the form of a condition: 'If you do so, then I will do so....' Secondly, the response to this condition is a noun-sentence.[121] Lastly, Allāh uses the pronoun before the verb, thus showing that He will of a surety substitute this money, for the verse states, '...then He will replace it...' and not, '...it will be replaced by Him.' These three ways of emphasizing the verse only show the importance and truthfulness of this statement, even though Allāh's statements are not in need of being emphasised!

Yet another verse that proves that spending in the way of Allāh increases one's wealth is the following:

ٱلشَّيْطَٰنُ يَعِدُكُمُ ٱلْفَقْرَ وَيَأْمُرُكُم بِٱلْفَحْشَآءِ
وَٱللَّهُ يَعِدُكُم مَّغْفِرَةً مِّنْهُ وَفَضْلًا وَٱللَّهُ وَٰسِعٌ عَلِيمٌ ﴿٢٦٨﴾

"*Shayṭān* threatens you with poverty and orders you to commit sins; Whereas Allāh promises you Forgiveness from Himself and Bounty, and Allāh is All-Sufficient for His creatures' needs, All Knowing." [Sūrah *al-Baqarah*, 268]

---

[120] *Tafsīr Ibn Kathīr* (3/595).

[121] In the Arabic language, all sentences are divided into noun sentences and verb sentences, depending on the first word of the sentence. Each type of sentence conveys a slightly different meaning, and each has its particular uses. In this particular case, the use of a noun-sentence adds an emphasis to the fact to be stated.

Ibn 'Abbās said in relation to this verse, "Two are from Allāh, and two are from *Shayṭān*. '*Shayṭān* promises you poverty' by telling you, "Don't spend your money! You are more in need of it!" And he also commands you 'with indecent deeds.' Yet 'Allāh promises you forgiveness from Him' for these sins that you do, 'and sustenance' by increasing your *rizq*!"[122] And Ibn al-Qayyim said, "(*Shayṭān's*) promise to make him poor is not because of him feeling sympathy for the person, nor because he desires some good for him! As for Allāh, then He promises His servant forgiveness for his sins, and His blessings by giving him more than what he spent, many times over, either in this world, or in this world and in the Hereafter."[123]

Of the evidences in the sunnah is what has been reported by Muslim in his *Ṣaḥīḥ* on the authority of Abū Hurayrah who said that the Prophet (ﷺ) said,

> "Allāh has said: 'O son of Ādam! Spend, I will spend on you!'"[124]

What a beautiful and simple ḥadīth! Spend in the way of Allāh, and Allāh will reward you by giving you more! What a simple way to increase our money! When we spend from our meagre resources, then the One who has the keys to the treasures of the Heavens and earth will spend upon us. This is a promise told to us by our Lord Himself. Is there any who is more truthful than Allāh? Nay, there is not. Yet, the problem is not in the promise; the problem is with ourselves, and how much we actually believe in this promise.

In fact, the Prophet (ﷺ) actually swore that charity does not decrease a person's money, as was quoted in a pervious ḥadīth:

> "Three matters, I will swear about them (that they are truthful) and I will narrate to you something, so memorize it:

---

[122] Reported by *al-Ṭabarī* (5/571).

[123] *Tafsīr al-Qayyim*, p. 168.

[124] Reported by Muslim (2/690).

Money will never decrease because of charity, and no person was ever wronged, and he was patient, except that Allāh will add to his honour, and no person opened for himself the door of asking (others for money), except that Allāh will open for him a door of poverty..." [125]

In another ḥadīth, the Prophet (ﷺ) said,

> "There is not a single day in which a servant wakes up except that two angels come down (from the Heavens). One of them says, 'O Allāh! Give to the one that spends a substitute (for what he has spent).' And the other one says, 'O Allāh! Give to the one that withholds (his money) destruction!'"[126]

In this ḥadīth, we learn that every single day two angels come down from the Heavens. One of them prays to Allāh to bless the one who spends for the sake of Allāh by giving him back what he spent, and more than that. The other one prays to Allāh to punish the one who is miserly by causing his money to be wasted and squandered on useless things, so that he has no money left. And it is well known that the prayer of the angels is a very blessed and holy prayer, and a prayer that Allāh generally responds to.

In another ḥadīth, we are shown the concern that the Prophet (ﷺ) had for the Companions, and his advice to them to spend in the way of Allāh. For it is narrated by Abū Hurayrah that the Prophet (ﷺ) said to Bilāl,

> "Spend, O Bilāl! And don't fear poverty from the Owner of the Throne!"[127]

---

[125] Reported by al-Tirmidhī (# 2325), who said it was *ḥasan Ṣaḥīḥ*, and Aḥmad (4/231). Al-Albānī agreed with al-Tirmidhī's verdict in his *Ṣaḥīḥ al-Targhīb* (# 14).

[126] Reported in al-Bukhārī (# 1442).

[127] Reported by al-Bayhaqī in his *Shuʿab al-Īmān,* and collected by al-Tibrizī in his *Mishkāt al-Maṣābīh* (# 1885), where al-Albānī declared it to be authentic in his checking of it (1/591).

In other words, spend in the way of Allāh, and don't presume that the Owner of the Throne will allow you to live in poverty if you spend in His cause. Is He not the *al-Ghanī*, the One who is Self-Sufficient in all His needs? Does He not provide the animals, and the birds, and the fish with their sustenance? In fact, is He not the One who provides the disbelievers their sustenance as well?

There are so many evidences from the Qur'ān and sunnah that prove that spending in the way of Allāh brings more *rizq* that they cannot all be mentioned in this small tract. Suffice to conclude this discussion by mentioning just one story that the Prophet (ﷺ) informed us about. The Prophet (ﷺ) said,

> "While a person was in an open area of land, he heard a voice in a cloud above him say, 'Water the garden of so-and-so!' So the cloud immediately departed, and started pouring its rain out on a rocky plain. A large crevice in the rocks collected all of this water. So the man followed the water (in its course), and he found a man standing in his garden, using an instrument to direct this water in different directions (to irrigate his garden). He said to him, 'O servant of Allāh! What is your name?' The man said, 'So-and-so,' the same name that he had heard in the clouds! Then the man asked him, 'O servant of Allāh! Why are you asking me my name?' So he responded, 'I heard a voice in the clouds – the same clouds that this water came from – saying, "Water the garden of so-and-so" with your name. What do you interpret this as (i.e., why do you think this happened)?' So he said, 'If you say this (i.e., if what you say occurred), then (the reason for this is that) I see what (crops) come out of it (this garden), and I give one third of it as charity, and I eat with my family one third of it, and I return one third of it (to cultivate more crops)'" and in another narration, it is reported that he said, '...and I give one third of it to the poor, and the beggars, and the wayfarers.'[128]

[128] Reported by Muslim (4/2288) and others.

So look at this man, who was living in a barren, rocky land, and see how Allāh blessed him with water to irrigate his crops! And ponder over the reason for this blessing, and see why Allāh favoured him, just because he gave of his money in the way of Allāh.

ix. Emigrating for the Sake of Allāh

Allāh, all Glory and Honour be to Him, has, in His wisdom, made emigration, or *hijrah*, one of the means of increasing one's sustenance. Therefore, it is essential that we understand the meaning of emigrating for the sake of Allāh, and the proof that this emigration brings about an increase in one's *rizq*.

The Meaning of Emigration, or 'Hijrah'

Emigration in the way of Allāh entails leaving a land in which a person cannot properly worship Allāh to a land where it is easier for him to worship Allāh. It means leaving the lands of the disbelievers, or of evil people, to the lands of the Muslims. It is essential for such an emigration to be sincerely for the sake of Allāh, and not for the sake of some worldly gain or benefit. The Prophet (ﷺ) said,

> "All actions are only by intentions, and every person will (be rewarded) for what he intended. So whoever emigrated for the sake of Allāh and His Messenger, then His emigration will be for Allāh and His Messenger. And whoever emigrated for the sake of some worldly gain that he would get, or for the sake of a woman to marry, then his emigration was for the reason that he did."[129]

---

[129] Reported by al-Bukhārī (# 1) and others.

The Proof that Hijrah Increases One's Sustenance

The proof for this fact is found in the statement of Allāh,

﴿ وَمَن يُهَاجِرْ فِي سَبِيلِ ٱللَّهِ يَجِدْ فِي ٱلْأَرْضِ مُرَٰغَمًا كَثِيرًا وَسَعَةً ۚ وَمَن يَخْرُجْ مِنۢ بَيْتِهِۦ مُهَاجِرًا إِلَى ٱللَّهِ وَرَسُولِهِۦ ثُمَّ يُدْرِكْهُ ٱلْمَوْتُ فَقَدْ وَقَعَ أَجْرُهُۥ عَلَى ٱللَّهِ ۗ وَكَانَ ٱللَّهُ غَفُورًا رَّحِيمًا ﴿١٠٠﴾

> "He who emigrates (from his home) in the cause of Allāh, will find on earth many dwelling places (*murāghama*) and plenty (to live by) (*sa'ah*). And whosoever leaves his home as an emigrant unto Allāh and His Messenger, and death overtakes him, then his reward is surely incumbent upon Allāh. And Allāh is ever Oft-Forgiving, Most Merciful." [Sūrah *al-Nisā*, 100]

In this verse, Allāh has promised whoever emigrates in His way two benefits and blessings. Firstly, he will find '*murāghama*', and secondly, '*sa'ah*.'

Al-Sa'adī explains,

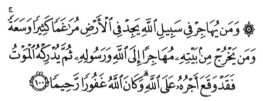

> This verse is encouraging *hijrah*, and exhorting to it, and explaining what blessings and benefits lie in it. For the True One has promised that whoever emigrates in His way, seeking His pleasure, that he will find '*murāghama*' and '*sa'ah*' in this world. And '*murāghama*' is a comprehensive word that implies all of the good of the religion, and '*sa'ah*' includes all of the good of this world. And this is because many people presume that *hijrah* leads to disunity after unity, and poverty after richness, and humility after honour, and hardships after ease. But that is not the case, for the believer, as long as he lives amongst the disbelievers, his religion will always be deficient.... But when he emigrates in the way of Allāh (to a Muslim land), then he will truly be able to establish the religion of Allāh, and fight the enemies of Allāh, and humiliate them and make them envious. For '*murāghama*' is a term that includes every factor that will infuriate the enemies of Allāh, from statements and actions. And he will

> also be blessed with extra sustenance, and this occurs exactly as Allāh has said![130]

So, the rewards of emigrating in the way of Allāh is that a person will be able to infuriate his enemies, and make them feel jealous of him, and this is contrary to what is expected. For, in general, when a person leaves his society and culture, and enters a foreign land, he remains a stranger in that land, never rising in status and wealth, while the people that he left behind continue to increase in their positions. But the one who emigrates for the sake of Allāh is blessed with the fact that Allāh rewards him with all types of rewards, monetary and otherwise, so much so that his enemies themselves wish that they were in his position!

x. Marriage

One of the ways in which a person is promised an increase in sustenance is through marriage. This will no doubt come as a surprise to many people. Perhaps this is because of the fact that one's poor financial situation is – in our times – the primary factor that *prevents* a person from marriage. And yet, the irony of the fact is that marriage is one of the easiest ways in which a person can guarantee an increase in sustenance from Allāh. Allāh states,

وَأَنكِحُوا۟ ٱلْأَيَٰمَىٰ مِنكُمْ وَٱلصَّٰلِحِينَ مِنْ عِبَادِكُمْ وَإِمَآئِكُمْ ۚ إِن
يَكُونُوا۟ فُقَرَآءَ يُغْنِهِمُ ٱللَّهُ مِن فَضْلِهِۦ ۗ وَٱللَّهُ وَٰسِعٌ عَلِيمٌ ﴿٣٢﴾

> "And marry those among you who are single (male and female) and (also marry) the pious of your (male) slaves and maid-servants (female slaves). If they be poor, Allāh will enrich them out of His Bounty. And Allāh is All-Sufficient for His creatures' needs, All-Knowing." [Sūrah *al-Nūr*, 32]

---

[130] *Tafsīr al-Saʿadī,* p. 160.

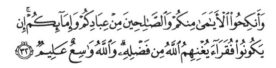

Al-Saʿadī says in explanation of this verse:

> "Allāh is commanding those who are in charge of the affairs of minors, and the slave-masters, to get those whom they are in charge of married, and this includes all who do not have a spouse, from men and women, virgins and widows. So it is obligatory on the close relative, and the one in charge of the orphan – all those whom he is obligated to support – to ensure that those that need to get married are married. And if they are obligated to get the people that they are in charge of married, then the obligation to get themselves married is even more apparent! ... And His saying, '...if they are poor...' meaning the husbands and the married couples, '...Allāh will enrich them out of His bounty...' so do not be prevented by what you might falsely assume that, once he gets married, he will become poor because of his family. And in this verse is a strong encouragement to get married, and a promise to the married one that he will become rich after poverty!"[131]

Al-Qurṭubī writes, commenting on this verse, "This means: let not the poverty of a man or a woman be a reason for not getting married. For in this verse there is a promise to those who get married for the sake of acquiring Allāh's pleasure and seeking refuge from disobeying Him (that Allāh will enrich him)...And in this verse is proof that it is allowed to marry a poor person. So one should not say, 'How am I going to get married when I don't have any money?' because his sustenance has been promised by Allāh. And the Prophet (ﷺ) married the woman who came to gift herself to him to a man who did not have except a single garment!"[132] He then writes, "So, since the greatest factor – in general – that prevents a person from getting married is that he does not have money, He promised that He would enrich the (married couple) from His bounties."[133]

---

[131] *Tafsīr al-Saʿadī*, p. 516.

[132] *Tafsīr al-Qurṭubi*, v. 12, p. 220.

[133] Ibid., (12/221).

And that is why we find that the Companions would encourage others to get married. Abū Bakr al-Ṣiddīq is reported to have said, "Obey Allāh in what He has commanded you to do by getting married; He will then fulfil His promise to you to make you rich." He then recited this verse.

And ʿUmar ibn al-Khaṭṭāb said, "Seek richness through marriage!" Likewise, ʿAbdullāh ibn Masʿūd said, "Find richness by getting married." And ʿAbdullāh ibn ʿAbbās said, "Allāh has commanded (the Muslims) to get married, and He has encouraged and enticed them for it. So He has commanded them to marry off their free-men and slaves (i.e., all those under their protection), and He has then promised them richness as a result (of this)." And it has been narrated that ʿUmar ibn al-Khaṭṭāb once remarked, "I have never seen anything stranger than a man who does not seek richness through marriage, even though Allāh has promised as a result of it (i.e., marriage) what He has promised: '...if they are poor, then Allāh will enrich them out of His Bounty!'"[134]

So, O Servant of Allāh! What is there now that prevents you from marriage? Is not this promise from Allāh sufficient for you? And do you not know that the Prophet (ﷺ) said,

> "Three people have a right upon Allāh that they should be helped: the one who desires to get married, seeking chastity; the slave that desires to be freed (by paying his master a pre-agreed amount of money); and the fighter in the way of Allāh."[135]

And in a ḥadīth with a slight weakness in it, it is reported that the Prophet (ﷺ) said,

---

[134] For all of these narrations, see *al-Durr al-Manthūr,* v. 5, pps. 80-81.

[135] Reported by al-Tirmidhī (1/311), who declared it *ḥasan ṣaḥīḥ,* al-Ḥākim (2/160), who declared it *Ṣaḥīḥ* and al-Dhahabī agreed with him, and others. It was also declared *ḥasan* by al-Albānī in *Ghāyat al-Marām* (# 210).

"Marry women, for they bring (a person) money."[136]

This promise of richness is not restricted upon the spouses. Allāh states, concerning children,

وَلَا تَقْتُلُوٓاْ
أَوْلَـٰدَكُمْ خَشْيَةَ إِمْلَـٰقٍ ۖ نَّحْنُ نَرْزُقُهُمْ وَإِيَّاكُمْ ۚ إِنَّ قَتْلَهُمْ كَانَ
خِطْـًٔا كَبِيرًا ﴿٣١﴾

"And kill not your children for fear of poverty. We provide for them and for you. Surely, the killing of them is great sin." [Sūrah *al-Isrā*, 31].

So do not fear poverty because of marriage, or because of children. Allāh, the *al-Razzāq*, will provide sustenance for them, just as He provided sustenance for their parents before them when they were young. And this is the promise of Allāh, so who is there that is more truthful than Allāh in His promise?

xi. Supporting Students of Islāmic Knowledge

Of the noble and effortless ways to increase one's *rizq* is by supporting students of knowledge, so that they can be free to study the religion of Islām to the best of their capabilities, without being impaired by trying to provide for their families.

---

[136] Reported by al-Ḥākim in his *al-Mustadrak* (2/161) and he considered it authentic, and al-Dhahabī agreed with him; al-Bazzār in his *Musnad* (2/149); al-Khaṭīb in his *Tarīkh Baghdād* (9/147), and others. However, Ibn Ḥajr pointed out that it has been narrated without mentioning the name of the Companion (i.e., *mursal*), which is one of the slightest forms of weakness in a ḥadīth (see his *Talkhīṣ al-Habīr*, 3/17). Therefore, this is a slightly weak ḥadīth; the only reason that it is being quoted is that it conforms with the verse in the Qur'ān.

The proof for this fact is found in a ḥadīth reported by al-Tirmidhī and al-Ḥākim, from Anas ibn Mālik, who staid, "There were two brothers (that lived) at the time of the Prophet (ﷺ). One of them would come to the Prophet (ﷺ), whereas the other one would seek his sustenance (by working). So the one who used to seek his sustenance complained to the Prophet (ﷺ) about his brother. The Prophet (ﷺ) replied,

> 'It is possible that you are provided your *rizq* because of him!'"[137]

In another narration, the brother said, "O Messenger of Allāh! My brother does not help me at all!" So the Prophet (ﷺ) replied,

> "But it is possible that you are provided your *rizq* because of him!"[138]

In other words, one of the brothers busied himself with obtaining money, whereas the other one constantly accompanied the Prophet (ﷺ), eagerly learning and studying as much as he could. However, the brother that studied with the Prophet (ﷺ) would rely on his other brother for food and sustenance. Hence, his brother complained to the Prophet (ﷺ) that he did not help him earn the money, yet shared with him the fruits of his own efforts, and ate and drank with him! So, the Prophet (ﷺ) informed him that it was possible that the reason he was so successful in obtaining money was due to the blessings of his other brother studying Islām. In other words, do not presume that your efforts are the sole reason for you being blessed with such abundant wealth; rather, instead of being ungrateful to your brother that he eats from 'your' money, it is very possible that your brother is the *source* of your blessings!

---

[137] Reported by al-Tirmidhī (# 2448), and al-Ḥākim in his *Mustadrak* (1/93), who said of it, "This ḥadīth is authentic according to the criterion of Muslim, and all of its narrators are trustworthy." Al-Dhahabī agreed with him, as did al-Albānī (see *Ṣaḥīḥ Sunan al-Tirmidhī,* 2/274).

[138] Reported by Ibn 'Abd al-Barr in his *Jāmi' Bayān al-'Ilm wa Faḍlihi* (# 121).

Mulla ʿAlī Qāri explained the statement, "It is possible that you are provided *rizq* because of him," by saying, "Meaning, 'I hope, or I fear, that you are given sustenance because of his blessings, and not that he is being fed due to your efforts, so do not consider it a favour to him that you feed him (rather it is a favour to you).'"[139]

Al-Ghazālī wrote, "(The person desiring to give charity) should seek out people that will be purified with his charity, such as people of knowledge, because this will help them to study. And seeking knowledge is the most noble act of worship, if the intentions are sincere. Ibn al-Mubārak would only give his charity to people of knowledge. He was asked, 'Why do you not broaden (your charity to other people)?' So he responded, 'I don't know any station, after the station of prophethood, that is more noble than the station of the scholars. So, if one of them is restrained by (not being able to) provide for himself, then he will not have any time for knowledge, nor will he teach others. So to provide them time to study and teach is better (than giving it to others).'"[140]

xii. Showing Kindness to the Poor

Of the ways that a person can increase his *rizq* is by showing mercy and kindness to the indigent and weak of society. This is because Allāh's blessings shower upon a society due to its poor and helpless people. The Prophet (ﷺ) said,

> "Is not the only reason that you are aided in victory (against your enemies) and provided with sustenance due to your weak?"[141]

Therefore, those that wish to achieve the help of Allāh, and be showered with sustenance and blessings, should be generous and

[139] *Mirqāt al-Mafātīḥ* (9/71).

[140] Taken from *Tafsīr al-Qāsimī* (3/250).

[141] Reported by al-Bukhārī (14/179).

kind to the weak of society; the down-trodden, meek and humble lower-classes that most others look down upon.

In fact, the Prophet (ﷺ) told us that if we wish to seek his pleasure, we will find it by pleasing this segment of society. He stated,

> "Find me amongst your weak, because the only reason that you are provided sustenance and aided in victory is because of your weak!"[142]

Mulla ʿAlī Qāri said, "'Find me amongst your weak,' meaning, 'Search for my pleasure by being kind and merciful to your poor.'"[143] The primary reason that Allāh provides us sustenance is due to the presence of weak and oppressed members of society; by being kind to them, Allāh will increase His *rizq* to us.

Therefore, even if we cannot afford to help them financially, at least we should treat them with compassion, love, and mercy, and not look down upon them with condescension and arrogance. For verily, it is not status and wealth that makes a person better then others, it is the *taqwa* of Allāh that does so.

xiii. Being Honest in One's Dealings

One of the ways in which a person procures Allāh's blessings is by being honest and truthful in his dealings and transactions with other people. When a person is conscious of Allāh, and strives to be honest and fair in his dealings with other people, Allāh will bless him in his transactions and cause them to be successful and fruitful. On the other hand, when a person is dishonest and does not care about disobeying Allāh when earning his wealth, Allāh

---

[142] Reported by Imām Aḥmad in his *Musnad* (5/ 198), Abū Dāwūd (# 2591), and al-Tirmidhī (# 1754), and others. It was declared authentic by al-Tirmidhī, al-Ḥākim, and al-Albānī (see *al-Silsilat al-Ṣaḥīḥah,* # 779).

[143] *Mirqāt al-Mafatīḥ,* (9/84).

then removes all His blessings from these transactions, and the person ends up losing in this world and the Hereafter.

The Prophet (ﷺ) said,

> "The two parties of a transaction have the right (to annul the contract) as long as they do not separate (from each other).[144] So, if they were truthful (to one another), and honest in explaining (the defects of an item), then they will be blessed in their transaction. But if they lied, and hid (the defects of an item) then the blessings of their transaction are destroyed!"[145]

So if both the parties were deceitful to each other, then there is no doubt that all the blessings from the transaction will be destroyed. However, the question arises: what if one of them was honest and the other one lied? Al-Ḥāfiẓ ibn Ḥajr said in response to this: "It is possible that the ḥadīth is taken on its apparent meaning, and that the evil effects of lying and cheating fall upon the transaction, even though (one of them was) truthful, so he will get his reward (for being truthful) and (the other one) was lying, so he will get the sin. It is also possible that this ḥadīth is specific to the one that cheated, not the other one (that was honest), and this opinion was the one that Ibn Abī Jamrah agreed with."[146] In any case, there is a danger that the blessings of the contract will be annulled even if one of the partners is dishonest, so beware!

---

[144] This means that, as long as the two parties of a contract are still physically together after agreeing upon a contract, either one of them is allowed to annul it (if he changes his mind) without any penalty. So, for example, if a person buys a car from another person, and then they remain talking for a while, it is allowed for the buyer (or the seller) to say, 'I've changed my mind. I don't think I want to buy (or sell) the car,' and then annul the contract by exchanging the two items again. However, once they physically separate from each other, then the contract becomes binding. This issue can be studied in greater detail in the books of *fiqh*.

[145] Reported by Muslim (#3836), Abū Dāwūd in his *Sunan* (# 3459), al-Nasā'ī (2/212) and others. Also see *Irwā al-Ghalīl* (# 1281).

[146] *Tuḥfat al-Aḥwadhī,* (4/375).

In another narration, the Prophet (ﷺ) said,

> "Allāh says: 'I am the third of two (business) partners, as long as one of them does not cheat his partner, but if he cheats him, then I leave from between them."

In another narration, one of the narrators, Rizīn, added at the end,

"...and *Shayṭān* comes."[147]

Shams al-Ḥaqq al-ʿAẓīmabādī said in explanation of this ḥadīth, "'I am the third of two partners' meaning that I am with them in protecting them, and blessing them; I guard their wealth and I give them sustenance and good from their transaction. And His saying, 'I leave them' means that all their blessings will be destroyed when My protection leaves them."[148] He then adds, "In this ḥadīth, there is evidence that partnerships are preferred, since blessings are given by Allāh to all the partners, and this is not the case when a person is by himself. This is because both of the partners will strive for the benefit of the other, and Allāh helps the servant, as long as the servant helps others."[149]

So honesty in dealing with one another in business transaction is a source of blessings, and insures that Allāh will help the partners

---

[147] Reported by Abū Dāwūd (# 3383) and others. The ḥadīth was declared authentic (*Ṣaḥīḥ*) by al-Ḥākim, and al-Dhahabī agreed with him (2/52), as did al-Mundhirī in his *Targhīb*. Al-Ḥāfiẓ Ibn Ḥajr did not give a verdict on it, but narrated it in his *Bulūgh al-Marām* (# 828), quoting al-Ḥākim's verdict on it, and also mentioned it in his *Talkhīs al-Habīr* (3/49), and so it appears that he did not consider it to be weak. Shaykh ʿAbdullāh al-Bassām considered it to be *ḥasan* in his *Tawḍīh al-Aḥkām* (4/136). However, ibn al-Qaṭṭān, al-Daraquṭnī and al-Albānī all ruled that the ḥadīth is weak (*al-Irwā*, # 1468). Even if this is the case, the previously-quoted ḥadīth is sufficient in this regards to prove this point.

[148] *ʿAwn al-Maʿbūd*, (9/237).

[149] Ibid, (9/237).

in their business and insure a profit for them. And what greater blessing can there be when Allāh Himself states that He will join their partnership, and help them? All of this is due to the sincerity and honesty of the business partners for one another.

It is noteworthy to realize that honesty and truthfulness bring about blessings in one's transactions in two manners. The first manner – and it is the greater of the two – is that Allāh has promised such a transaction to be fruitful and blessed. He has even called Himself their partner, so how can an undertaking in which one of the partners is *al-Razzāq* be devoid of fruit? The second manner is that a person, by being honest, will establish his reputation amongst the people as a trustworthy and respectable businessmen. His other partners will spread good words about him, and thus businessmen will strive to make him their partner and to engage in transactions with him. They will be at ease in dealing with him, and their hearts will be inclined towards choosing him instead of others. This is in contrast to the dishonest cheat. Not only does *Shayṭān* become his partner – as narrated in one wording of the ḥadīth – but also his reputation is destroyed. He will be abandoned by other traders and businessmen, and left to his own. And all of this is well-known and experienced in all cultures! So look, therefore, at the blessings that honesty and truthfulness bring to a business, and strive to please your Lord and not be dishonest with His servants.

xiv. Making the Hereafter One's Main Concern

Of the blessings that Allāh gives the believers when they set their primary goal to be the Hereafter is that He provides for them in this world as well. When the slave realizes the ultimate goal and strives to achieve it, Allāh provides all the sustenance and resources needed while the slave is traversing the path to reach this goal.

Once Zayd ibn Thābit was with Marwān, the leader of the city, when he went to visit ʿAbd al-Raḥmān ibn ʿUthmān ibn ʿAffān. ʿAbd al-Raḥmān said, "Nothing caused him to come here, at this hour, except a question that he wants to ask." So he asked him (what the matter was). He replied, "He (meaning Marwān) asked us about matters that we heard the Prophet (ﷺ) say.[150] I heard the Prophet (ﷺ) say,

> 'Whoever puts this world as his only (and primary) goal, then Allāh will divide his affairs for him, and He will place poverty right before his very eyes, and nothing will come to him of this world except that which was already written (i.e., pre-destined) for him. But whoever made the Hereafter his goal, then Allāh will gather his affairs for him, and He will place richness in his heart, and the world will come to him conquered and submissive.'"[151]

In another narration, the wording is:

> "Whoever makes the world his (only) concern, and his only cause of grief – on it he places his sight (and goal), and only it he intends – then Allāh will place between his very eyes poverty, and He will disperse his matters, and nothing will come to him of it except that which was written for him. But whoever sets the Hereafter as his (only) concern, and his only cause of grief – on it he places his sight (and goal), and only it he intends – then Allāh will place richness (and self-

---

[150] In other words, Zayd is saying, 'I wanted to confirm with you whether this ḥadīth was heard by you or not, and whether I was correct in informing Marwān about it.' And this is just one of hundreds of examples that shows the care and concern with which the Companions used to narrate ḥadīth of the Prophet (ﷺ).

[151] Reported by Ibn Mājah (# 4105). Al-Būṣayrī said in his *Zawā'id* (4/425) that its chain is authentic, and al-Albānī agreed with him (*al-Ṣaḥīḥah,* # 950). Also reported by al-Tirmidhī (2/76) with a different chain, and he did not comment on it, but the preceding narration strengthens it in any case.

> sufficiency) in his heart, and He will gather his affairs for him, and the world will come to him while it is humiliated."[152]

So the one who does everything for this world, such that his eating, sleeping, and actions are all intended to procure worldly benefit – every cause of happiness to him is related to this world, and every distress is due to a worldly loss – then such a person will never find richness. It might be possible that his material possessions are many, but when his heart is not content with what he has, he will always consider himself poor. His whole life will be wasted in trying to amass what he considers true richness, yet, every time he gains more, his greed demands that he work yet harder. So he neither benefits from the work that he has done, nor does he benefit from the money that he has earned.

As for the one who dedicates his life in order to achieve the ever-life of the Hereafter – his every move is for the sake of Allāh – then such a person will be blessed with sustenance without him even tiring himself in search of it. Additionally, he will be content with what he has been given, and 'true richness is contentment.' He will not feel the need to belittle himself in front of others in search for more sustenance, but rather will be satisfied with whatever Allāh has given him.

Al-Imām al-Sindī said, in explanation of the phrase '…and the world will come to him while it is humiliated':

> "This means that it will come 'overpowered and conquered'. So the point is that whatever *rizq* is written for a servant will come to him no matter what, except that if he strives for the Hereafter, then it will come to him without any effort, whereas if he strives for this world, then it will come to him with difficulty, and after great pains. So the one who seeks the Hereafter has combined between this world and the Hereafter, because the only reason for gaining money is to

---

[152] See *al-Ṣaḥīḥah*, (# 949).

achieve comfort in this world, and this will be achieved by a person who strives for the Hereafter. As for the one who strives for this world, then he will lose this world and the Hereafter, because in this world he will undergo extreme hardship and exert great efforts to achieve it (and as for the good of the Hereafter, he will never get it since he did not strive for it in the first place). So what benefit is there in all this money if there is no comfort with it?"[153]

Another evidence for this point is the ḥadīth narrated by ʿAbdullāh ibn Masʿūd, who stated that the Prophet (ﷺ) said,

> "Whoever made all his concerns one concern – the concern of the Hereafter – then Allāh will suffice him his worldly (needs). And he who multiplied his concerns – the various concerns of this world – then Allāh does not care in which valley he is destroyed."[154]

So the wise man is he who realizes that all goals are useless and trivial, except for the goal of Paradise. Therefore, he removes all other desires from his heart, and he concentrates on the one and only worthwhile goal: that of pleasing Allāh by worshipping Him. Such a person will be blessed by Allāh, and his needs will be taken care of. And how can it be that the needs of the servant not be taken care of by the Lord, especially when the lord is *al-Karīm* (The Ever-Generous), *al-Mannān* (The One who Gives freely and Constantly)?

As for the one whose heart is filled with multiple goals – for he wants to hoard as much money as he can, and build fancy houses

---

[153] *Hāshiyah Sunan Ibn Mājah*, (4/425).

[154] Reported by Ibn Mājah (# 4016) and al-Ḥākim (4/329) who said that it was authentic. However, al-Dhahabī disagreed with him, and also al-Būṣayrī, who said, 'Its chain is weak' (1/167). And it is as they said; however, the ḥadīth has supporting evidence, including the preceding narrations, and therefore al-Albānī declared it to be acceptable (*ḥasan*) in his checking of *Mishkāt al-Maṣābīḥ* (# 263).

and mansions, and marry beautiful women, and own the most luxurious of items, and try to fulfil every whim and caprice that his heart yearns for – then such a person is no servant to Allāh, and Allāh does not care what happens to him. When the servant does not fulfil the rights of the Creator, then how can he expect the Creator to fulfil His rights to the servant? Al-Sindī states, "The phrase: 'Allāh does not care in which valley he is destroyed' signifies that Allāh does not help him in anything."[155]

The ḥadīth that was quoted earlier can also be used as supporting evidence for this section. Abū Hurayrah stated that the Prophet (ﷺ) said,

> "Allāh says, 'O Son of Ādam! Take time out to constantly worship me, I will fill your chest with richness, and remove your poverty. And if you do not do so, I will make your hands filled with occupation, and will not remove your poverty.'"[156]

xv. Striving to Achieve the Goal

The religion of Islām is the only perfect religion. It combines for its followers the benefits of this world and the benefits of the Hereafter. So, after a Muslim has taken all the necessary steps in order to earn money – by making his intentions pure, and having *taqwa* of Allāh, and being honest in his dealings, etc. – he then must strive physically to achieve this goal. It is not feasible that he will obtain *rizq* without striving for it, as is assumed by certain groups that allege to put their trust in Allāh, and claim that their *rizq* will come to them without them doing anything![157] Rather, the

---

[155] *Hāshiyah Sunan Ibn Mājah*, (4/425).

[156] Reported by al-Tirmidhī (# 2583), Ibn Mājah in his *Sunan* (# 4159), and others. Al-Albānī declared it to be authentic in his *Ṣaḥīḥ Sunan al-Tirmidhī*, (2/300).

[157] The reference here is to the *Sūfīs* who claim that true *tawakkul* involves leaving all means of reaching the goal, and instead worshipping Allāh by innovated methods and means.

true Muslim is one who, after making sure that his intentions are pure, strives his utmost to achieve the goal, all the while ensuring that the methods and paths that he uses are sanctioned by Allāh and not prohibited by Islām.

The Qur'ān clearly points to this concept. In one verse, Allāh states,

هُوَ ٱلَّذِى جَعَلَ لَكُمُ
ٱلْأَرْضَ ذَلُولًا فَٱمْشُوا۟ فِى مَنَاكِبِهَا وَكُلُوا۟ مِن رِّزْقِهِۦ ۖ وَإِلَيْهِ ٱلنُّشُورُ

> "He it is, Who has made the earth subservient to you (i.e., easy for you to walk, live and cultivate, etc.), so walk in the path thereof and eat of His provision, and to Him will be the Resurrection." [Sūrah *al-Mulk*, 15]

In another verse, Allāh states,

عَلِمَ أَن سَيَكُونُ مِنكُم مَّرْضَىٰ ۙ
وَءَاخَرُونَ يَضْرِبُونَ فِى ٱلْأَرْضِ يَبْتَغُونَ مِن فَضْلِ ٱللَّهِ ۙ

> "He knows that there will be some sick amongst you, and others (that) travel in the land, seeking Allāh's bounty." [Sūrah *al-Muzzammil*, 20]

In this verse, Allāh states that He is aware of the situation of His slaves. Some will be sick, others fighting in the way of Allāh, and yet others who travel through various lands, trying to seek the blessings of Allāh, through business and trade, and other means. In this verse, the seeking of Allāh's bounty is directly related to travelling in search of it, thus showing that it is necessary to strive to achieve this goal.

Allāh also mentions the wisdom behind the creation of animals, for He states,

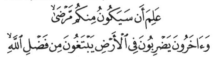

وَٱلْأَنْعَٰمَ
خَلَقَهَا ۗ لَكُمْ فِيهَا دِفْءٌ وَمَنَٰفِعُ وَمِنْهَا تَأْكُلُونَ
﴿٥﴾ وَلَكُمْ فِيهَا جَمَالٌ حِينَ تُرِيحُونَ وَحِينَ تَسْرَحُونَ ﴿٦﴾
وَتَحْمِلُ أَثْقَالَكُمْ إِلَىٰ بَلَدٍ لَّمْ تَكُونُوا۟ بَٰلِغِيهِ إِلَّا بِشِقِّ
ٱلْأَنفُسِ ۚ إِنَّ رَبَّكُمْ لَرَءُوفٌ رَّحِيمٌ ﴿٧﴾

"And the cattle, He has created them for you; in them there is warmth (warm clothing), and numerous benefits, and of them you eat. And wherein is beauty for you, when you bring them home in the evening, and you lead them forth to pasture in the morning. And they carry your loads to lands that you could not reach except with great trouble to yourselves. Truly, your Lord is full of Kindness, Most Merciful." [Sūrah *al-Naḥl*, 5-7]

Therefore, these animals help us in transporting our goods and merchandise to far-away lands, so that we can increase in our profit and supplement our income.

In yet another clear indication of this point, Allāh mentions that the wisdom behind the creation of the day and night is so that mankind can engage itself in earning money – through *ḥalāl* means – during the day. The fact that the entire earth is lit up around us during the day greatly facilitates a person's quest for sustenance. Allāh states,

وَجَعَلْنَا ٱلَّيْلَ وَٱلنَّهَارَ ءَايَتَيْنِ ۖ فَمَحَوْنَآ ءَايَةَ ٱلَّيْلِ وَجَعَلْنَآ ءَايَةَ
ٱلنَّهَارِ مُبْصِرَةً لِّتَبْتَغُوا۟ فَضْلًا مِّن رَّبِّكُمْ وَلِتَعْلَمُوا۟ عَدَدَ
ٱلسِّنِينَ وَٱلْحِسَابَ ۚ وَكُلَّ شَىْءٍ فَصَّلْنَٰهُ تَفْصِيلًا ﴿١٢﴾

"And We have appointed the night and the day as two signs (of Ours). Then, We have extinguished the sign of the night while We have made the sign of day bright, that you may seek bounty from your Lord, and that you may know the number of the years and the reckoning. And we have explained everything with full explanation (in detail)." [Sūrah *al-Isrā*, 12]

In another verse,

وَمِن رَّحْمَتِهِۦ جَعَلَ لَكُمُ ٱلَّيْلَ
وَٱلنَّهَارَ لِتَسْكُنُوا۟ فِيهِ وَلِتَبْتَغُوا۟ مِن فَضْلِهِۦ وَلَعَلَّكُمْ تَشْكُرُونَ

"It is out of His Mercy that He has put for you night and day, that you may rest therein (during the night) and that you may seek of His Bounty (during the day), and in order that you may be grateful." [Sūrah *al-Qaṣaṣ*, 73]

Allāh calls attention to the fact that this is one of the greatest miracles of creation:

وَمِنْ ءَايَـٰتِهِۦ مَنَامُكُم بِٱلَّيْلِ
وَٱلنَّهَارِ وَٱبْتِغَآؤُكُم مِّن فَضْلِهِۦٓ ۚ إِنَّ فِى ذَٰلِكَ لَـَٔايَـٰتٍ
لِّقَوْمٍ يَسْمَعُونَ ﴿٢٣﴾

"And among His miracles is the sleep that you take by night and by day, and your seeking of His Bounty. Verily, in that are indeed signs for a people who listen." [Sūrah *al-Rūm*, 23]

Allāh also points out the miraculous nature of the ship, for it rides the ocean without sinking, and is able to carry passengers and materials on it. Of the wisdom behind this is,

وَهُوَ ٱلَّذِى
سَخَّرَ ٱلْبَحْرَ لِتَأْكُلُوا۟ مِنْهُ لَحْمًا طَرِيًّا وَتَسْتَخْرِجُوا۟
مِنْهُ حِلْيَةً تَلْبَسُونَهَا وَتَرَى ٱلْفُلْكَ مَوَاخِرَ فِيهِ
وَلِتَبْتَغُوا۟ مِن فَضْلِهِۦ وَلَعَلَّكُمْ تَشْكُرُونَ ﴿١٤﴾

"And He it is Who has subjected the sea (to you), that you eat thereof fresh, tender meat (i.e., fish), and that you bring forth out of it ornaments to wear. And you see the ships ploughing through it, that you may seek (thus) of His Bounty (by transporting the goods from place to place) and that you may be grateful." [Sūrah *al-Naḥl*, 14]

And also,

رَّبُّكُمُ ٱلَّذِى يُزْجِى لَكُمُ ٱلْفُلْكَ
فِى ٱلْبَحْرِ لِتَبْتَغُوا۟ مِن فَضْلِهِۦٓ ۚ إِنَّهُۥ كَانَ بِكُمْ رَحِيمًا ﴿٦٦﴾

"Your Lord is He Who drives the ship for you through the sea, in order that you may seek of His Bounty. Truly! He is Ever Most Merciful towards you." [Sūrah *al-Isrā*, 66]

Lastly,

ٱللَّهُ ٱلَّذِى سَخَّرَ لَكُمُ ٱلْبَحْرَ لِتَجْرِىَ ٱلْفُلْكُ فِيهِ بِأَمْرِهِۦ وَلِتَبْتَغُوا۟ مِن
فَضْلِهِۦ وَلَعَلَّكُمْ تَشْكُرُونَ ﴿١٢﴾

"Allāh: it is He Who has subjected to you the sea, that ships may sail through it by His Command, and that you may seek of His Bounty, and that you may be thankful." [Sūrah *Al-Jāthiyah*, 12]

So the animals that we ride, and the ships that we sail, and that land that we traverse, and the day that we work in: all are but blessings from Allāh in order for us to utilize them in our search for wealth. These blessings need to be utilised in order to gain yet more blessings.

Allāh mentions the great blessings He had given to the tribe of Quraysh by blessing them with two journeys, one in the winter to Yemen, and one in the summer to Syria. These two journeys were meant solely for the purpose of trade, and was one of the causes for the superiority of the Quraysh over other tribes. Allāh reminds them of this blessing, and also reminds them of what the blessing necessitates,

لِإِيلَـٰفِ قُرَيْشٍ ﴿١﴾ إِۦلَـٰفِهِمْ رِحْلَةَ ٱلشِّتَآءِ وَٱلصَّيْفِ
﴿٢﴾ فَلْيَعْبُدُوا۟ رَبَّ هَـٰذَا ٱلْبَيْتِ ﴿٣﴾ ٱلَّذِىٓ أَطْعَمَهُم
مِّن جُوعٍ وَءَامَنَهُم مِّنْ خَوْفٍۭ ﴿٤﴾

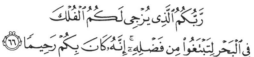

> "(It is a great grace and Protection from Allāh), for the accustomed security of the Quraysh. Their accustomed security (in) the caravan of winter (to the south), and in the summer (to the north, without any fear). So let them worship (Allāh) the Lord of this House (the Ka'bah). (He) Who has fed them against hunger, and has made them safe from fear." [Sūrah *Quraysh*, 1-4]

In fact, even in the religious obligation of Ḥajj, Allāh allows for the believers the opportunity to engage in trade and transactions, and in this there is a great blessing from Allāh. Never do so many people, from so many different parts of the world, come together, and this phenomenon, without a doubt, is a great boost to trade. Here is a trader coming with his merchandise from a far away land, and there is a buyer who would otherwise never have the opportunity to purchase this item at all, or to purchase it at such a reasonable price. This is one of the wisdoms of allowing a pilgrim to engage in business, as Allāh says,

لَيْسَ عَلَيْكُمْ جُنَاحٌ أَن
تَبْتَغُوا فَضْلًا مِّن رَّبِّكُمْ ۚ فَإِذَا أَفَضْتُم مِّنْ
عَرَفَاتٍ فَاذْكُرُوا اللَّهَ عِندَ الْمَشْعَرِ الْحَرَامِ ۖ
وَاذْكُرُوهُ كَمَا هَدَاكُمْ وَإِن كُنتُم مِّن قَبْلِهِ
لَمِنَ الضَّالِّينَ ﴿١٩٨﴾

> "There is no sin on you if you seek the Bounty of your Lord (during pilgrimage by trading). But when you leave 'Arafāt, remember Allāh at the Holy Sanctuary (of Muzdalifah). And remember Him as He has guided you, for verily, you were, before, of those who were astray." [Sūrah *al-Baqarah*, 198]

So all of these verses prove that it is obligatory that a person strives his utmost to achieve the goal, and not sit back and pretend to have *tawakkul* in Allāh, without taking any action to achieve the goal. Allāh is the One that created the day and the night, so that we can strive during the day to earn our living, and rest in peace during the night. He is the One who has given us control over the land, so that we can travel through its mountains and hills, and cultivate its plains and forest, and harvest its crops. He has given us control over animals, so that we can travel on mounts to different countries, and transport goods which otherwise would have been impossible. He has given us control over the ships, upon which we ride the oceans to strange lands, and so that we can engage in trade and transaction. All of this He has blessed us with in order that we may increase in our quest for Allāh's blessings, and therefore increase in our worship of Him.

We must realize that the One in whom we must put our trust is the One that has commanded us to strive our utmost to achieve our goals. He is the Giver of our desires, and the path to achieve that desire. So the wise one is he who realizes that, just as the goal is achieved by the blessings of Allāh, so too is the path to achieve that goal. Allāh is the creator of the goal and the means to attain that goal. ʿUmar ibn al-Khaṭṭāb stated, "Let not one of you sit back from earning, and say, 'O Allāh! Give my sustenance!' For verily you know that gold and silver does not fall down from the skies in rain."[158]

So every person should take up a profession, and learn it, study it, and practice it, so that he can earn a pure income. And this studying in and of itself can become an act of worship if he makes his intentions pure. ʿUmar also said, "I see a man that impresses me, so I ask, 'Does he have a profession (through which he earns money)?' So if they say, 'No,' then he falls from my eyes (and I do not respect him)."[159]

And let us not forget that one of the primary ways that we should strive to attain our *rizq* is to pray sincerely to Allāh to bless us with sustenance that is pure and blessed. Allāh states,

---

[158] Reported by al-Ghazālī in his *Iḥyā* (2/62).

[159] *Kanz al-ʿUmmāl*, (4/123).

وَقَالَ رَبُّكُمُ ٱدْعُونِىٓ أَسْتَجِبْ لَكُمْ ۚ إِنَّ ٱلَّذِينَ يَسْتَكْبِرُونَ عَنْ عِبَادَتِى سَيَدْخُلُونَ جَهَنَّمَ دَاخِرِينَ ﴿٦٠﴾

"And your Lord said: Call out to Me, I will of a surety respond to you. Verily! Those who are too arrogant to worship Me will surely enter Hell in humiliation." [Sūrah *Ghāfir*, 60]

This is a general verse that promises a response to all prayers, as long as they are permissible. In a more explicit verse, Allāh states,

وَلَا تَتَمَنَّوْا۟ مَا فَضَّلَ ٱللَّهُ بِهِۦ بَعْضَكُمْ عَلَىٰ بَعْضٍ ۚ لِّلرِّجَالِ نَصِيبٌ مِّمَّا ٱكْتَسَبُوا۟ ۖ وَلِلنِّسَآءِ نَصِيبٌ مِّمَّا ٱكْتَسَبْنَ ۚ وَسْـَٔلُوا۟ ٱللَّهَ مِن فَضْلِهِۦٓ ۗ إِنَّ ٱللَّهَ كَانَ بِكُلِّ شَىْءٍ عَلِيمًا ﴿٣٢﴾

"And wish not for the things in which Allāh has made some of you to excel others. For men there is reward for what they have earned, (and likewise) for women there is reward for what they have earned, and ask Allāh of His Bounty. Surely, Allāh is Ever All-Knower of everything." [Sūrah *al-Nisā*, 32]

And that is why Prophet ʿĪsa, *ʿalayhi salām*, when he prayed to Allāh to bless him and his disciples with a table of food, prayed,

ٱللَّهُمَّ رَبَّنَآ أَنزِلْ عَلَيْنَا مَآئِدَةً مِّنَ ٱلسَّمَآءِ تَكُونُ لَنَا عِيدًا لِّأَوَّلِنَا وَءَاخِرِنَا وَءَايَةً مِّنكَ ۖ وَٱرْزُقْنَا وَأَنتَ خَيْرُ ٱلرَّٰزِقِينَ ﴿١١٤﴾

"O Allāh, our Lord! Send us from heaven a table spread (with food) that there may be for us – for the first and the last of us – a festival, and a sign from You; and provide us sustenance, for You are the Best of sustainers." [Sūrah *al-Mā'idah*, 114]

And the Prophet Ibrāhīm prayed to Allāh to bless Makkah:

وَإِذۡ قَالَ إِبۡرَٰهِـۧمُ رَبِّ ٱجۡعَلۡ هَٰذَا بَلَدًا ءَامِنٗا وَٱرۡزُقۡ
أَهۡلَهُۥ مِنَ ٱلثَّمَرَٰتِ مَنۡ ءَامَنَ مِنۡهُم بِٱللَّهِ وَٱلۡيَوۡمِ ٱلۡأٓخِرِۚ قَالَ وَمَن كَفَرَ
فَأُمَتِّعُهُۥ قَلِيلٗا ثُمَّ أَضۡطَرُّهُۥٓ إِلَىٰ عَذَابِ ٱلنَّارِۖ وَبِئۡسَ ٱلۡمَصِيرُ ١٢٦

"And (remember) when Ibrāhīm said, 'My Lord, make this city (Makkah) a place of security, and provide its people with fruits, such of them as believe in Allāh and the Last Day.' He (Allāh) answered: 'As for him who disbelieves, I shall leave him in contentment for a while, then I shall compel him to the torment of the Fire, and evil indeed is that destination!'" [Sūrah al-Baqarah, 126]

Ibrāhīm also prayed:

رَّبَّنَآ إِنِّيٓ أَسۡكَنتُ مِن ذُرِّيَّتِي بِوَادٍ غَيۡرِ ذِي زَرۡعٍ عِندَ بَيۡتِكَ
ٱلۡمُحَرَّمِ رَبَّنَا لِيُقِيمُواْ ٱلصَّلَوٰةَ فَٱجۡعَلۡ أَفۡـِٔدَةٗ مِّنَ ٱلنَّاسِ
تَهۡوِيٓ إِلَيۡهِمۡ وَٱرۡزُقۡهُم مِّنَ ٱلثَّمَرَٰتِ لَعَلَّهُمۡ يَشۡكُرُونَ ٣٧

"O our Lord! I have made some of my offspring to dwell in a valley with no cultivation, by Your Sacred House (the Ka'bah at Makkah), in order, O our Lord, that they may offer prayers perfectly, so fill some hearts among men with love towards them, and provide them with fruits so that they may give thanks." [Sūrah *Ibrāhīm*, 37]

And the Prophet (ﷺ) prayed for his servant Anas ibn Mālik,

"O Allāh! Increase his money and children, and bless him in whatever you give him."

Many years later, Anas remarked, "There is no one from the Anṣār that has more money that I do, and my daughter Umaynah informed me that when Ḥajjāj attacked Baṣra (and killed many of its inhabitants) over one hundred a twenty of my offspring were

[160] Reported by al-Bukhārī (# 202) and others.

amongst those buried."[160] Therefore, pray to Allāh to increase your *rizq*, just like the prophets before you prayed.

So, dear reader, once you realize that *rizq* must be strived for, and will not come miraculously out of the skies, then what are you waiting for? Obey the commandant of Allāh, in which He tells the believers to pray, and

فَإِذَا قُضِيَتِ ٱلصَّلَوٰةُ فَٱنتَشِرُوا۟ فِى ٱلْأَرْضِ
وَٱبْتَغُوا۟ مِن فَضْلِ ٱللَّهِ وَٱذْكُرُوا۟ ٱللَّهَ كَثِيرًا لَّعَلَّكُمْ تُفْلِحُونَ

> "...then, when the prayer has finished, disperse throughout the land, and seek from the bounties of Allāh, and remember Allāh frequently, so that you may be successful." [Sūrah *al-Jumuʿah*, 10]

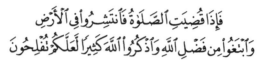

Conclusion

The Prophet (ﷺ) said,

> "If the son of Ādam were to flee from his *rizq* the way that he flees from death, then of a surety his *rizq* would catch him just as death does."[161]

So seek your wealth in beautiful and permissible means, like the Prophet (ﷺ) said,

> "Seek this world in a beautiful manner, for every person's affairs have been made easy for him, according to what he has been created for."[162]

In other words, whatever is decreed for a person will come to him, and he will find it easy to achieve what was pre-destined for him. So let every person seek his wealth in the most beautiful and perfect manner, for he will only be able to get whatever has been written for him.

And realize, O Muslim, that disobeying Allāh will not bring about happiness in this life or the Hereafter. Earning one's wealth through *ḥarām* brings more grief than pleasure, and more harm than good. And disobeying Allāh is one of the reasons that a person's *rizq* can be diminished. It has been narrated that the Prophet (ﷺ) said,

---

[161] Reported by Abū Nu'aym in his *Ḥilya* (7/90) and others. Al-Albānī declared it *ḥasan* in *al-Ṣaḥīḥah* (# 952).

[162] Reported by Ibn Mājah (2/3) and al-Ḥākim (2/3) who declared it authentic, and al-Dhahabī and al-Albānī agreed with him (*al-Ṣaḥīḥah* # 898).

> "Indeed, the servant (of Allāh) is denied some sustenance (that was otherwise written for him) because of a sin that he does."[163]

And beware, O Muslim, of greed and avarice! Allāh has censured the one who loves to hoard and amass wealth, without giving the rights that are due upon it. Likewise, the Prophet (ﷺ) said to one of the Companions,

> "O Ḥakīm! This money is green and luscious, so he who takes it with a generous soul (i.e., his heart is not attached to it), then he will be blessed with it. But he who takes it with a greedy soul, then he will not be blessed with it, for he is like the one that eats but is never satisfied. And know that the giving hand is better than the receiving one!"[164]

This short treatise is concluded with a ḥadīth that summarizes the essence of seeking Allāh's sustenance and gaining more wealth.

ʿAbdullāh ibn Masʿūd narrated that the Prophet (ﷺ) said:

---

[163] Reported from the *musnad* of Thawbān by Ibn Mājah (# 4022), and al-Būṣayrī said, "Its *isnād* is good (*ḥasan*);" al-Ḥākim (3/493), who stated that it was an authentic (*Ṣaḥīḥ*) ḥadīth, and al-Dhahabī agreed with him; al-Ṭabārani in his *al-Mu'jam al-Kabīr* (2/100, # 1442); al-Baghawī in his *Sharḥ al-Sunnah* (13/6, # 3418) and others. However, al-Albānī stated (in *al-Ṣaḥīḥah* # 154) that this wording of the ḥadīth is not authentic, as the narrator from Thawban – ʿAbdullāh ibn Abī al-Jaʿad – is *majhūl al-ḥāl* , or 'unknown' (except that Ibn Ḥibbān mentioned him in his *al-Thiqāt*). Perhaps those who considered the ḥadīth authentic took into account that many scholars, such as al-Dhahabī and Ibn Kathīr, differentiated between the various levels of unknown (*majhūl*) narrators, and considered the level of the Successors (*tabiʿīn*) to be acceptable as long as other conditions were met, and Allāh knows best.

[164] Reported, with various wording, by al-Bukhārī (# 6427), Muslim (# 2742), al-Tirmidhī (# 2191) and others. See *Ṣaḥīḥ al-Targhīb wa al-Tarhīb*, (# 806).

O Mankind! The Holy Spirit (Jibrīl) has whispered in my soul that no person shall die until his time be complete, and his sustenance be finished. So fear Allāh, and seek your sustenance in a beautiful (i.e., permissible) manner. And let not any of you – when his sustenance appears to be delayed in arriving – try to seek it through disobeying Allāh! For verily, what Allāh has (with Him) can never be obtained except through obedience to Him. [165]

[165] Reported by al-Ḥākim (2/4) who declared it authentic, and al-Dhahabī agreed with him; Ibn Ḥibbān (# 1084 of the *Iḥsān* edition); and al-Baghawī in his *Sharḥ al-Sunnah*, and it is recorded in *al-Mishkāt* (# 5300). Al-Albānī also considered it to be authentic in his *Bidāyat al-Sūl*, p. 59, and *Takhrīj Mushkilāt al-Faqr*, p. 20.

Select Bibliography

- Al-Isfahānī, Rāghib. *Mufradāt al-Qurān al-Karīm.* Ed. by Safwān Dawudi. Dār al-Qalam, Damascus. 1997 A.H.

- Elahi, Faḍl. *Mafātīḥ al-Rizq fī Ḍaw al-Kitāb wal-Sunnah.* Idārah Tarjumān al-Qurān, Pakistan. 1417 A.H.

- Suyuṭī, Jalāl al-Dīn. *Uṣūl al-Rifq fī al-Ḥuṣūl ala al-Rizq* (published as an article in Majallāh al-Ḥikmah, v. 3, Muḥarram 1415 A.H., pps. 249-269).

- Al-Tabrīzī, Muḥammad ibn ʿAbdillāh. *Mishkāt al-Maṣābīḥ.* Ed. By Muḥammād Nāsir al-Dīn al-Albānī. Al-Maktab al-Islami, Beirut. 1405 A.H.

- Al-Tawīl, Aḥmad ibn Aḥmad. *Ṭalab al-Rizq bayn al-Ḥalāl wa l-Ḥarām.* Dār al-Muslim, Riyadh. 1994 C.E.